# The Good and Bad Science of Autism

## Dr. Neil Walsh & Dr Elisabeth Hurley

Autism West Midlands • UK

# Foreword by Jonathan Shephard

**Chief Executive, Autism West Midlands**

At Autism West Midlands our emphasis is on improving the lives of people with autism and their families. It's a highly practical approach, relying on a large number of dedicated staff. At the same time, we train and explain: we train our own staff, and we train other organisations including local authorities, GPs, and police forces.

In our training we explain what autism is, and we deal with aspects of life with autism: challenging behaviour; sexuality; employment issues; autism and siblings. This book takes explanation to a different level. It is an introduction, principally for the general reader, to the science of autism. Scientific understanding of autism has improved dramatically in the past two decades, but we are only at the start of a long journey. Myths about autism still abound, and there are many unvalidated and sometimes dangerous ideas about autism and how it can be addressed. We passionately believe that timely specialist intervention can bring major improvements in the quality of life of someone with autism, and can improve skills, confidence, social interaction, and in many cases employment prospects. At the same time, we believe that autism is a life-long condition, and that claims of "cure" are giving false hopes.

This book charts the developing understanding of autism, from its first identification more than 60 years ago. It deals in detail with the controversial issue of whether autism is increasing. It looks at the influence of the media, which is often deeply unhelpful. And it explains why a rigorous scientific approach is so important: where good science is absent, bad science will fill the gap - and there is too much bad science around.

The authors, Neil Walsh and Elisabeth Hurley, both have doctorates in genetics (Neil Walsh) and neuroscience (Elisabeth Hurley). As noted, they are writing for the general reader, rather than for the scientific community, but the book does provide, even for academics, a valuable general introduction to the good and bad science of autism.

# How to read this book

We have designed this book to be easy to read and simple to follow using a colour coding system:

## Summary sections

- Dark purple pages appear at the beginning of each chapter
- These pages summarise the main text within a chapter
- Each chapter ends with a dark purple summary box. This box contains bullet points which highlight the key points of the chapter

**If you want an overview of this book and don't want to delve too deeply, read the dark purple sections.**

## "Focus On"

- Pink sections appear at points throughout the book
- These pages go into detail about an aspect of the preceding chapter, and are designed to give you a greater understanding of the text
- Some examples of topics covered are "Sex differences in autism" and "An introduction to molecular genetics"

### Explanation bubbles

These turquoise bubbles appear throughout the text. They offer an explanation of key concepts used in the chapter. If an explanation bubble is available for a word, the word is written in turquoise and the bubble will be nearby.

# Contents

# Chapter 1:
# Introduction

In recent years, there has been a dramatic increase in the rate of autism diagnosis in the population. This has generated a lot of public and professional interest in autism accompanied by a surge in research into the biological basis of this enigmatic condition. Autism is highly complex and diverse and its exact causes remain elusive. Despite this, scientific investigation has made good progress towards explaining its biological underpinnings.

Along with good scientific research that has moved our understanding forward, autism unfortunately has a history of being accompanied by bad science. This can be traced all the way back to when autism was first described in the 1940s when it was thought be a psychological condition resulting from poor parenting. The discovery that autism has a genetic basis has largely dispelled this idea but there are still many misconceptions and pseudoscientific ideas surrounding autism which are sometimes fuelled by poor science communication in the media.

Being able to distinguish the good science in autism from the bad requires having some understanding of the scientific method. Good science involves hypothesising a possible explanation for a problem, making predictions about what should happen if the hypothesis is correct and carefully testing these predictions. If the results do not support the hypothesis it must either be discarded or modified and retested. If the results do support the hypothesis it must be replicated multiple times, ideally by independent research groups who test the hypothesis in different ways. This process makes science a powerful tool because it is self-critical and is always subject to review by others in the scientific community.

The purpose of this book is twofold. Firstly, an overview of our current scientific understanding of autism will be presented along with the methods that were used to generate this knowledge – the 'good science' of autism. Secondly, the 'bad' science will be considered – the misconceptions, anecdote-driven beliefs and pseudoscience that have held back the public understanding of this complex and many-faceted condition.

Few issues in modern medicine have received as much public and professional interest as autism. Driven by the discovery that rates of autism appear to be dramatically increasing in the population, there has been a huge surge of research into the biological basis of autism in recent years. In parallel to this scientific interest the public awareness of autism has also greatly increased, with numerous popular books, websites and television programmes exploring this condition. However, there is often a significant divide between the public's understanding of the nature and causes of autism and views of the scientific community. Alongside the 'good' autism science - the careful accumulation of genetic and other evidence-based research to build a picture of how autism is caused and develops - there is a large amount of 'bad' science. The latter involves misinformation based on speculation and anecdote which is driven by emotion rather than reason. Bad science can lead to incorrect conclusions about autism and can divert research funding away from understanding its true causes. In order to improve the public understanding of the science behind autism it is important to distinguish between good and bad lines of inquiry and the evidence that relates to these.

The history of bad autism science goes back a long way. Following its identification as a distinct childhood disorder in 1943 autism was interpreted for decades as being, basically, a psychological condition. The explanation for autism was that it was caused by parents being emotionally unresponsive to their children, leading to childhood psychosis. In the absence of scientific evidence, psychiatric interpretations led to the promotion of the 'refrigerator mother' hypothesis which proposed that mothers were essentially to blame for the autism in their children by their failure to nurture them adequately. This resulted in a stigma being attached to autism which presumably compounded the difficulties involved in raising a child with autism. The discovery in the 1970s that autism has a largely genetic basis disproved the 'refrigerator mother' hypothesis. Although the associated stigma has been largely abandoned, some countries continue to attach it to parents of children with autism[1].

Modern science has a formidable array of tools and approaches that can be used to study autism but, despite years of research and millions of pounds of research funding, no clear answer has been found for its genetic and environmental causes. The symptoms of autism are highly diverse. The classical idea of autism, put forward by the psychiatrist Leo Kanner[2], as representing people who are largely uncommunicative with severe intellectual impairments, has been expanded over time. Today autism encompasses a broad spectrum of traits and now includes people who are often highly intelligent but possess unusual behavioural traits and experience difficulties in social understanding.

It has become clear from scientific research that autism is a highly complex condition and that its causes will be difficult to unravel. When a child appears to develop normally for the first couple of years of their life and then begins to show signs of autism, such as forming an emotional barrier with their parents, it seems only natural that the parents will want clear answers as to why this has happened. Unfortunately, as science has not provided any simple explanation for autism, in their search for answers many members of the public turn to alternative and popular - but scientifically unsupported - explanations.

The age of the internet has facilitated unprecedented access to a wealth of information about a variety of medical conditions and disabilities. In theory, people therefore have the potential to inform themselves on numerous subjects previously accessible only to academics and experts. However, much of the information available is unfiltered and pseudo-scientific, consisting of speculation, anecdotes and conjecture. This is certainly the case in relation to autism: many websites promote the now scientifically discredited idea that vaccines given to young children are responsible for causing autism. In the UK and United States this has led to reduced levels of vaccination and an increase in the cases of dangerous childhood diseases such as measles. This trend has been exacerbated by the mainstream media who have often promoted pseudoscientific ideas about the causes of autism and provided uncritical platforms for the spokespeople of the anti-vaccination movement. The media also commonly misrepresent genuine science by exaggerating modest results for the sake of a more gripping news story.

Because autism is a developmental disorder with a strong genetic link, it has no cure. There are a small number of scientifically validated interventions for autism which are not intended to 'cure'

## Peer-review:

The process by which a scientific study, typically presented in the form of a research paper, is assessed for its methodological quality and contribution to scientific knowledge prior to publication. The editor of the journal in which the paper is to be published receives the research paper from the authors and sends it on to a number of experts in the field who review the research paper and evaluate it. The editor then makes a decision about whether to publish the research paper based on the experts' feedback.

autism as such but instead aim to improve quality of life by enabling people with autism to deal better with challenging social environments. However, in recent years, a multitude of unscientific treatments for autism have sprung up. Many of these 'treatments' are promoted with exaggerated claims of effectiveness based on personal anecdotes, but are rarely supported by any empirical evidence. They are often very costly and in some cases have been shown to be hazardous for health. It is important for parents and carers of people with autism to be able to critically evaluate these claims and be aware of the available supporting evidence.

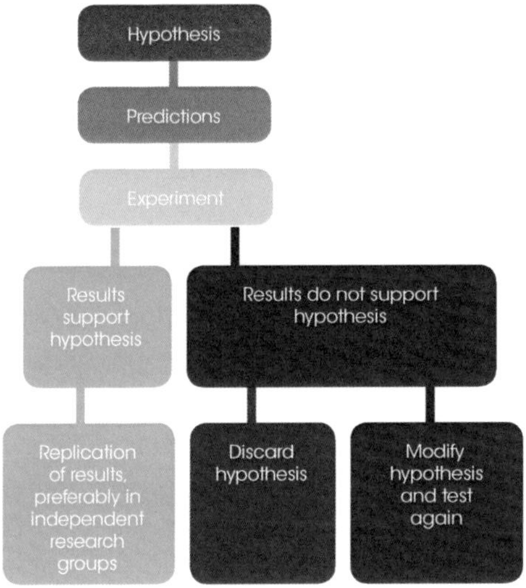

This book endeavours to help make scientific research more accessible and to steer a course through the good and the bad of autism research. Good science involves hypothesising a possible explanation for a problem, making predictions about what should be observed if the hypothesis is correct and then testing these predictions through careful experimentation and comparisons (Figure 1). If the results of the experiment do not support the hypothesis, it must be either discarded or modified and tested again. If the results do support the hypothesis, then before it can be fully accepted the results must be replicated multiple times, ideally by independent research groups who test the hypothesis in different ways. This is the key to why science is such a powerful tool - it is rigorous and highly self-critical. An explanation for something may sound plausible and convincing but unless it has been tested and is supported by evidence it should not be accepted as fact. The critical nature of the scientific method means that alternative possible explanations for problems are always considered. In order for scientific findings to be accepted and published they must pass a strict process of peer-review where other experts in the field critique and evaluate the results to ensure that they are valid and substantial. The peer-review process is not perfect and studies are sometimes published which contain mistakes. However, once published, studies can be reviewed by the scientific community who may confirm or contest

**Figure 1**

Hypothesis → Predictions → Experiment

Results support hypothesis / Results do not support hypothesis

Replication of results, preferably in independent research groups / Discard hypothesis / Modify hypothesis and test again the results in their own publications.

One consequence of the scientific method is that our understanding of the world is continually revised and updated, with old ideas being replaced with new in the light of fresh evidence. Rather than this being a weakness of science, it is actually a strength: theories can be added to and improved on provided they are supported by the facts. In contrast, the practitioners of pseudoscience can be highly resistant to change. They are often convinced that their ideas are correct and no amount of contrary evidence can convince them otherwise.

Gaining a full understanding of a complex condition like autism is a lengthy process of exploration. Scientists build on previously published research, re-evaluating and expanding on it. Over the course of many research projects and the collaborative efforts of numerous scientists a picture is gradually developing of the nature and causes of autism. There has been much progress into understanding the genetic basis of autism and how it affects the development of the brain. Some progress has also been made in uncovering the environmental factors that may contribute to autism and how these may interact with genetic predispositions to increase the likelihood of someone having autism. Additionally science-based interventions have been developed to improve the quality of life of people with autism. Unfortunately, given the poor quality of science communication by the mainstream media and the large amount of misinformation present on the internet and other sources, it can be difficult to separate out the 'good' science from the 'bad'. This book attempts to address this problem by presenting a review of the current state of the scientifically validated autism research, followed by a description and analysis of the pseudoscientific side to autism research and how it has been represented in the media.

## Summary points

- Autism is receiving increasing public and scientific attention.
- It is a highly complex and diverse condition and its exact causes remain elusive.
- Scientific research has made good progress towards understanding the biology of autism.
- There are also many misconceptions and pseudoscience surrounding autism.
- It is important to be able to evaluate claims made about autism and separate the 'good' science from the 'bad'.

**References**

1 Taylor Dyches, T, Wilder, L K, Sudweeks, R R, Obiakor, F E and Algozzine, B (2004) "Multicultural issues in autism." *Journal of Autism and Developmental Disorders*, 34(2), pp. 211–222.

2 Kanner, L (1943) "Autistic disturbances of affective contact." *Nervous Child*, 2, pp. 217–250.

# Chapter 2:
# What is autism?

In general terms autism is classified as a neurodevelopmental disorder: an impairment of the development of the central nervous system. Over the years, the definition of autism has been expanded to reflect our increased understanding of the complexities of the condition. It is becoming increasingly common to use the term Autism Spectrum Disorders (ASDs) to encompass autistic disorder, Asperger syndrome and pervasive developmental disorders-not otherwise specified (PDD-NOS) and this will be reflected in the publication of the newest version of the American Psychiatric Association (APA) Diagnostic and Statistical Manual of Mental Disorders, version 5 (DSM-5). The World Health Organisation's (WHO) own manual, the International Classification of Diseases, version 10 (ICD-10) will continue to distinguish these disorders as separate diagnoses, at least until it is revised in 2015.

Despite the differences in how autism is classified the main difficulties experienced by people who have autism are similar. The commonly experienced difficulties are in social interaction and interpretation of behaviour. There may be repetitive and restrictive behaviours and there may be special interests of unusual intensity. Some people with autism experience difficulties in verbal communication – they may not communicate verbally or they may repeat what is said to them. Conversely some people with Asperger syndrome can be highly articulate. There is a lot of variation in how people experience these difficulties reflecting the complexity and variability of autism.

This chapter will provide an introduction to how autism is defined, classified and diagnosed and will also describe the important role that research plays in increasing our understanding of the nature of autism.

Since it was proposed as a distinct disorder by Kanner in 1943, concepts used to define and explain autism, along with its classification and diagnosis, have changed dramatically. Early diagnostic criteria were more stringent and restricted to the more extreme cases of autism. The discovery in the 1970s that autism has a strong genetic basis led to it being recognised as a biomedical, rather than a psychiatric, condition and since then the definition of autism has broadened over time[1]. Today, autism is recognised not as a single disorder but as a range of disorders that are placed under a single label.

In general terms autism is classified as a neurodevelopmental disorder: an impairment of the development of the central nervous system. Signs of autism appear in the first three years of life, with parents observing that their child displays temperamental extremes, lack of eye contact or unusual responses to visual stimuli. People with autism have problems communicating with others and have lifelong difficulties dealing with novel situations and changing routines. Autism is described as a syndrome, rather than a disease: it has no specific biological marker but is instead defined as a collection of signs and symptoms that occur together, without reference to the underlying cause of these traits. There are also a number of other medical conditions which can occur alongside autism, such as epilepsy[2] and gastrointestinal problems[3].

There are two widely used modern international classification systems that set out the definition of, and diagnostic criteria for, autism. The first is the Diagnostic and Statistical Manual of Mental Disorders (DSM), published by the American Psychiatric Association (APA) in the USA. The second is the International Classification of Diseases (ICD) published by the World Health Organization. The current version of the DSM – DSM-IV-TR - will be replaced by a new version - DSM-5 – in May 2013, while the current version of the ICD – ICD10 – is due for revision in 2015.

In DSM-IV-TR and ICD-10 autism is defined and diagnosed in a similar way, based on the observation of behavioural traits. It is grouped under an umbrella of disorders affecting communication, social interactions and compulsive behaviours collectively named pervasive developmental disorders (PDDs). PDDs include autistic disorder (narrowly defined autism) and a number of other subtypes such as Asperger syndrome and pervasive developmental disorders- not otherwise specified (PDD-NOS). Together with autistic disorder, these are sometimes regarded as a continuum that represents different degrees of severity of the same overall condition. Also, in recent years, there is increasing recognition of what is termed the 'broader autism phenotype', where some people display a pattern of relatively mild symptoms of autism that are recognisable, but lower than those diagnosable as autism[4].

Because the characteristic behaviours of autism vary considerably from person to person placing someone into a distinct category of autism can be quite problematic. The diagnosis of autism is typically performed by specialists who use a system of standardised testing and clinical evaluation. Two of the main diagnostic and assessment tools that are used are the Autism Diagnostic Interview - Revised (ADI-R) and the Autism Diagnostic Observation Schedule (ADOS), both developed in the early 1990s. The diagnosis of autistic disorder (the most severe type) depends on there being major difficulties in three behavioural categories, with early symptoms appearing before the age of three:

1. Abnormalities in relation to reciprocal social interactions such as lack of eye-contact, problems with empathy and in initiating and maintaining conversations.

2. Delays in developing language and inabilities to grasp nuances of language such as sarcasm and humour and difficulties in interpreting body language.

3. Repetitive and restrictive behaviours such as hand-flapping, and narrow interests, particularly those involving categorisation (an obsession with sports statistics for example).

Beyond these three defining criteria there is a lot of variability in the traits that people with autism express which can range from mild to debilitating. However all three criteria are required for a diagnosis of autistic disorder. Furthermore, a high proportion of people with autism also experience differences in how they process sensory information[5]. People with autism can be hypo- or hyper-sensitive to any of their senses (vision, taste, hearing, touch, smell, balance and awareness of self in space).

A person can be diagnosed as high-functioning or low-functioning depending on whether they score higher or lower than 70 on the non-verbal intelligence test (NVIQ). The main difference between Asperger syndrome and high-functioning autistic disorder is that people with Asperger syndrome do not have clinical language problems, although they do display symptoms in the other two diagnostic categories. Because there are many similarities between high-functioning autistic disorder and Asperger syndrome, it has been argued that it may be unnecessary to differentiate between these two conditions[6].

People with PDD-NOS do not fit into the categories of either autistic disorder or

Asperger syndrome but they do have some clear symptoms of autism such as repetitive and restrictive behaviours or problems with social interaction.

There are a number of other PDDs such as Rett syndrome, a rare disorder that is more common in females than in males. Rett syndrome has some similar features to autistic disorder such as lack of speech and stereotypical hand movements but there are important differences such as head growth developing unusually slowly[7]. Another rare PDD is childhood disintegrative disorder (CDD) where the infant's development is normal for at least two years but after this time they develop social and communication problems similar to those associated with autism but typically even more severe[8].

PDDs are sometimes referred to as autism spectrum disorders (ASDs), a term that reflects the various degrees of severity and combinations of symptoms that can occur within and among these conditions. ASDs will become a clinical diagnostic term from May 2013 when the new version of the DSM will introduce it as a single diagnosis which will encompass autistic disorder, Asperger syndrome and PDD-NOS. ICD-10 is due for revision in 2015 and it is currently not known whether it will also adopt the term ASDs or keep its current format. In DSM-5, the new diagnostic criteria will still cover the main areas which are affected in people with autism but will alter the way that these criteria are grouped to reflect the current knowledge of how ASDs present. As such, ASDs will be characterised by difficulties in two main areas:

1. Social communication and social interaction.

2. Repetitive and restrictive behaviours and sensory difficulties.

The forthcoming changes in diagnostic criteria reflect years of research into the previous diagnostic criteria and how to improve specificity and sensitivity[9,10]. However, given the little knowledge of the underlying causes of these conditions, it is possible that autistic disorder and other ASDs such as Asperger syndrome are distinct entities that overlap only in relation to the behavioural traits that they have in common. The question of whether the various ASDs are really distinct from one another, or whether they simply represent variations of the same condition, has a number of implications for research and treatment. If they are truly distinct then they each may have a different cause which could affect the search for biological markers for early identification, or influence decisions about what interventions would be most effective. Only by understanding the biology of autism can these issues be resolved and this can only be accomplished through scientific research[11,12].

As well as there being a large amount of variation in the traits exhibited by people with autism, there are also differences in the timing of the onset of symptoms. In most infants subtle signs of autism appear very early in life and progress into clearer symptoms by about two years of age[1]. However, in about 20 - 30% of infants, development appears to proceed normally for the first 18 - 24 months and then a regression to symptoms of autism occurs which includes the loss of previously acquired social and language skills[13].

It is clear that autism is a complex condition, with a range of characteristics and levels of severity, which defies a simple definition. Concepts of autism continue to evolve in both the medical community and in the general public. For example, in some published studies, the authors have preferred to use the term 'autism spectrum conditions' instead of 'autism spectrum disorders' as they felt that this would be less stigmatising to people with autism[14]. The emphasis on a 'condition' rather than a disorder reflects the positive cognitive attributes that people with autism often display. It is understood today that autism can exist among people of all intelligence levels and it has been argued that autism-like traits represent a valid aspect of the human condition and should not be regarded as requiring a treatment or cure. Given the broad range of terminology that is employed in describing diagnosed autistic conditions, autistic disorder, Asperger syndrome and PDD-NOS will be referred to as 'autism' for the remainder of this book.

## Summary points

- Autism is a set of neurodevelopmental disorders defined by their symptoms.
- The two main classification systems used for autism are the DSM-IV-TR and ICD-10.
- In the current classification systems autism includes autistic disorder, Asperger syndrome and PDD-NOS.
- There are three behavioural categories relating to autism: social interaction, language and repetitive/restrictive behaviour. People with autism often also have sensory difficulties.
- An updated version of the DSM – DSM-5 – is due to be released in May 2013.
- DSM-5 will group autistic disorder, Asperger syndrome and PDD-NOS under Autism Spectrum Disorders.
- There can be a lot of variation within these categories and also in the timing of onset of symptoms.

### References

1  Volkmar, F, Chawarska, K and Klin, A (2005) "Autism in infancy and early childhood." *Annual Review of Psychology*, 56, pp. 316–336.

2  Danielsson, S, Gillberg, I C, Billstedt, E, Gillberg, C and Olsson, I (2005) "Epilepsy in young adults with autism: a prospective population-based follow-up study of 120 individuals diagnosed in childhood." *Epilepsia*, 46(6), pp. 918–923.

3  Adams, J B, Johansen, L J, Powell, L D, Quig, D and Rubin, R A (2011) "Gastrointestinal flora and gastrointestinal status in children with autism - comparisons to typical children and correlation with autism severity." *BMC Gastroenterology*, 11, p. 22.

4  Bailey, A, Palferman, S, Heavey, L and Le Couteur, A (1998) "Autism: the phenotype in relatives." *Journal of Autism and Developmental Disorders*, 28(5), pp. 369–392.

5  Marco, E J, Hinkley, L B N, Hill, S S and Nagarajan, S S (2011) "Sensory processing in autism: a review of neurophysiologic findings." *Pediatric research*, 69(5 Pt 2), p. 48R–54R.

6  Toth, K and King, C H (2008) "Asperger's syndrome: diagnosis and treatment." *American Journal of Psychiatry*, 165(8), pp. 958–963.

7  Chahrour, M and Zoghbi, H Y (2007) "The story of Rett syndrome: from clinic to neurobiology." *Neuron*, 56(3), pp. 422–437.

8  Volkmar, F R and Rutter, M (1995) "Childhood disintegrative disorder: results of the DSM-IV autism field trial." *Journal of the American Academy of Child & Adolescent Psychiatry*, 34(8), pp. 1092–1095.

9  Frazier, T W, Youngstrom, E A, Speer, L, Embacher, R, et al. (2012) "Validation of proposed DSM-5 criteria for autism spectrum disorder." *Journal of the American Academy of Child and Adolescent Psychiatry*, 51(1), pp. 28–40.e3.

10  Mandy, W P L, Charman, T and Skuse, D H (2012) "Testing the construct validity of proposed criteria for DSM-5 autism spectrum disorder." *Journal of the American Academy of Child and Adolescent Psychiatry*, 51(1), pp. 41–50.

11  Leventhal, B L (2012) "Lumpers and splitters: who knows? Who cares?" *Journal of the American Academy of Child and Adolescent Psychiatry*, 51(1), pp. 6–7.

12  Ozonoff, S (2012) "DSM-5 and autism spectrum disorders—two decades of perspectives from the JCPP." *Journal of child psychology and psychiatry, and allied disciplines*, 53(9), pp. e4–6.

13  Barger, Brian D, Campbell, Jonathan M and McDonough, Jaimi D (2012) "Prevalence and Onset of Regression within Autism Spectrum Disorders: A Meta-analytic Review." *Journal of Autism and Developmental Disorders*.

14  Baron-Cohen, S, Scott, F J, Allison, C, Williams, J, et al. (2009) "Prevalence of autism spectrum conditions: UK school-based population study." *British Journal of Psychiatry*, 194(6), pp. 500–509.

# Chapter 3:
# Is autism becoming more common?

Autism was originally believed to be rare, occurring in about four cases per 10,000 children. In the UK today, it has been estimated that around 1.1% of the population has autism. This increase has sparked discussions of whether we could be in the midst of an autism "epidemic" and whether some novel environmental factor may be contributing to the rise in the number of autism diagnoses. It is more likely, however, that the observed increase is due to improvements in autism awareness coupled with instances of diagnostic substitution, a phenomenon which occurs when one diagnosis is changed for another that is more appropriate.

Evidence for the diagnostic substitution hypothesis comes from observations that as the number of cases of autism have increased the number of cases of other mental illnesses has decreased – some of those previously considered to be mentally ill are now known to have autism. Furthermore, a true increase in autism prevalence would be apparent in increases in the number of children being diagnosed compared to the number of adults diagnosed. However, recent epidemiological studies have shown no difference in the prevalence of autism in adults compared to children. Therefore, although it is possible that there has been a small genuine increase in the prevalence of autism due to an as yet unidentified factor, the main reason for the increase in autism prevalence seems to be due to increases in autism awareness and improved diagnosis.

This chapter will describe the rise in diagnosed cases of autism, the possible reasons for this increase and discuss the research undertaken to explore this surprising phenomenon.

There has been an evolving view of autism over the years from a narrowly defined psychiatric disorder to being recognised as a complex set of traits with several layers of variability and degrees of expression. This coincides with a startling trend that is being observed - the number of new diagnoses of autism is dramatically increasing.

Autism was originally believed to be rare, occurring in about four cases per 10,000 children. Over the last 20 years this estimate has steadily increased and recent studies of prevalence, drawn from multiple sources and population groups, have reported rates of autism of about 1.1%[1]. This means that autism is considerably more common than Down's Syndrome, for example. The dramatic rise in the rate of autism has been widely reported in the popular press and has sparked debates about whether there is an autism 'epidemic' taking place[2]. There are basically two possible general explanations (which differ in the level of support they have):

**1) The increase in autism diagnoses may be due to a change in environmental conditions.**
Concerns about environmental agents that may be contributing to a rise in autism have focused on various types of vaccines, particularly those containing the preservative thimerosal, as somehow 'triggering' the onset of autism in young children[3]. As discussed later in detail, extensive research on this issue has provided strong evidence against a role for vaccines in autism prevalence. However, it remains at least intuitively possible that there may be some, as yet unidentified, aspect of the changing environment that we live in that may be contributing to an increased prevalence of autism.

**2) The rise in observed** prevalence **is mostly or entirely due to changes in the way that autism is defined and identified.**

**Prevalence:**
A term used in epidemiology to describe how common a condition is in the population at a particular point in time.

The broadening of the definition of autism over time to include Asperger syndrome means that there is now a wider collection of symptoms available for diagnosis, including subtler traits not previously considered to be strict signs of autism. This means that more people now fall under the diagnostic criteria for autism. One consequence of this is that some children who were previously diagnosed as having other conditions, such as language disorders, are now diagnosed with autism. This is an example of "diagnostic substitution"[4]. As more and more diagnoses are being re-characterised as autism the prevalence of autism rises. We shall now consider this in more detail.

One prediction that arises from the diagnostic substitution hypothesis is that the increase in autism prevalence in recent years will have been accompanied by a corresponding decrease in the prevalence of other disabilities. There is some evidence that this is the case. For example, one study performed in the United States investigated the prevalence of disabilities among children in special needs education from 1984-2003. It was found that increases in autism prevalence were significantly associated with decreases in the number of recorded cases of intellectual disabilities over this time[6].

Other studies have attempted to determine whether the broadening of diagnostic criteria is responsible for the increase in autism prevalence by applying modern criteria for autism to people who had previously been diagnosed with other behavioural and intellectual disabilities. Bishop et al. (2008) applied contemporary diagnostic criteria for autism to a group of adults who had been diagnosed with language disorders as children[4]. Developmental language disorders are often diagnosed when a child has major problems acquiring spoken language and as such have a degree of overlap with the symptoms of autism. Bishop et al. (2008) found that a number of these adults would have been diagnosed with autism by today's diagnostic criteria[4]. Although the number of people used in this study was small this research adds weight to the diagnostic substitution hypothesis.

**Diagnostic substitution:** When one diagnosis is replaced by a different diagnosis because of improved understanding and/or changing diagnostic criteria.

If changing diagnostic criteria are largely responsible for the increase in identified cases of autism then when the same criteria are applied over time the prevalence of autism should remain the same. Chakrabarti & Fombonne (2005) repeated a study they had previously performed several years before of autism prevalence among children in Stafford. They rigorously applied the same methods for autism diagnosis they had previously used to a group of children born during a later period. The prevalence figure for the later study remained the same which argued against a genuine increase in the incidence of autism[6].

Another way of attempting to determine if there is a real increase in the occurrence of autism is to compare the prevalence of autism among young and old age groups using the same diagnostic criteria. A real increase should be reflected by a higher rate of autism in the younger group. A large-scale survey of autism prevalence rates in the UK by the NHS in association with the University of Leicester in 2009 was the first major study into the prevalence of autism among adults. It found that the autism prevalence rate among adults was the same as for children suggesting that the real incidence of autism is not increasing[7].

Other than broadening of the diagnostic criteria, a number of social factors may have contributed to the increase in diagnoses of autism in the population. Epidemiological studies of autism have played a role in increasing awareness among the medical community and this has led to improvements in screening and surveillance and to the early detection of autism in the population, as well as improvements in available services. Medical practitioners are more informed about autism and so are able to make better diagnoses. There is a recognition that early intervention can improve the quality of life of people with autism and this provides an incentive to identify autism at as young an age as possible. Also, awareness of autism has increased in the general public and there appears to be less of a stigma associated with autism than in the past. Parents may therefore be more likely to take their child for a diagnostic assessment. As a result of these factors,

**Epidemiology:**
A branch of medicine that deals with the occurrence and distribution of disease within populations and also addresses the origin and causes of disease epidemics.

rather than the numbers of people with autism increasing, there may simply have been an underestimate of the numbers of people with autism in the past.

One of the interesting patterns to emerge from epidemiological studies of autism prevalence is the association between autism and socioeconomic status. Some conditions, such as infant mortality and heart disease, are more common in families with lower socioeconomic status[8]. However, in an opposite pattern to this, there is a greater likelihood of autism among families with a better income or education. It is not believed that socioeconomic status has any direct effect on the risk of autism. Instead, it is thought that the explanation for this pattern lies in the fact that families from wealthier backgrounds typically have better access to medical care and information. This means that affluent parents may be more likely to recognise signs of autism in their child and bring them for an assessment. As a result, although children from socioeconomic backgrounds of high- and low-status **are both equally likely to have autism,** children from the wealthier families are more likely to receive a diagnosis[9].

For example, a study on trends in autism diagnoses in California found that children from wealthier families were more likely to be diagnosed with autism[10]. However, it was also found that children from poorer families that lived in affluent areas were much more likely to receive an autism diagnosis than children from equally poor families that lived in poorer neighbourhoods. In more affluent areas, there was a better infrastructure for the communication of information relating to autism among parents and better awareness of the available service systems for autism diagnosis and treatment. It appears that sociological factors and in particular community level resources can be important factors in determining the likelihood of a child receiving a diagnosis of autism.

In Asia, with the exception of Japan, there appears to be resistance to the idea that autism is highly common. In these countries there is a tendency, perhaps due to cultural stigmas, to diagnose children who would be considered to have autism by European standards as having psychological conditions, such as reactive attachment disorder, the cause of which is largely blamed on the children's mothers[11,12]. A recent study in South Korea conducted a survey for undiagnosed cases of autism in the general population using international criteria and found the prevalence rate to be 2.64%, or more than twice the previously estimated prevalence[13]. Many of the children identified as being on the autism spectrum were functioning relatively well in mainstream classrooms.

Overall, the available evidence strongly suggests that there has not been a genuine major increase in the occurrence of autism; the increasing prevalence of autism is likely to be due instead to diagnostic substitution and increases in awareness and screening. However, it remains possible that there may have been some real increase in the number of people with autism on top of these factors. This may be due to some as yet unknown environmental factors but their contribution to the overall number of cases of autism is likely to be small. As yet there is no direct evidence for such a connection, although one cannot be ruled out. A number of large-scale studies are currently underway to search for possible environmental factors associated with autism. These will be discussed in more detail in Chapter 6. Awareness of the high rate of autism in the population has led to better educational services, earlier diagnosis, better treatment and less social stigma for people with autism. It has also contributed to the increase in research funding into the causes of autism and its biological underpinnings. In particular, the genetics of autism has become an area of intense research due to the discovery that autism has a strong genetic basis.

## Summary points

- The number of new diagnoses of autism is dramatically rising.

- This is mainly due to changing environmental conditions or changes in the way that autism is defined and diagnosed. However, we cannot rule out that unknown environmental factors may also contribute to this increase.

- Epidemiological studies suggest that diagnostic substitution and increases in awareness explain most of the increase in prevalence.

- It is possible that there has been some genuine increase in autism due to an as yet unidentified factor or factors.

# Focus on: Sex differences in the expression of autism

One interesting pattern that has emerged from studies of the prevalence of autism is that boys are four times more likely to be diagnosed with autism than girls[9]. The factors that are responsible for this pattern have not been determined but it is possible that genetic factors may make a contribution. For example, oxytocin and vasopressin are genetically determined peptides (similar to proteins) that are produced in the central nervous system and regulate behaviour, in particular social interactions[14]. The genes that underlie these peptides have been associated with autism and there are sex differences in their levels of activity[14]. Mutations in genes such as these may contribute to the risk of developing autism and explain some of the sex differences in autism prevalence.

Another potential explanation for the sex difference observed in autism prevalence could relate to the levels of sex hormones that are expressed in the developing brain. Sex hormones such as testosterone, which are regulated differently in males and females, can have a range of effects on behaviour and the development of the brain by altering the activity of neurochemicals[14]. There is a genetic component to the regulation of sex hormones and there is evidence that genes involved in sex hormone function are associated with autism[15].

Although genetic differences may be responsible for a greater occurrence of autism in males compared to females, it is also possible that non-biological factors, such as cultural expectations and social differences in the upbringing of boys and girls, could affect differences in the diagnosis of autism between the sexes and lead to an under-reporting of autism in females. Behavioural traits such as shyness and sensitivity, which are common in people with autism, may also be associated with 'femaleness' and less likely to be regarded as abnormal when observed in girls. Social groups composed of girls may be more inclusive of a member who has autism compared to a parallel group composed of boys, and a girl with autism may be less likely to 'stand out from the crowd'. As a result of these issues parents may be less likely to bring their daughters for a diagnostic test for autism.

It is also possible that autism may be expressed differently in males and females. Girls with autism may not be as severely affected as boys in relation to social interactions and may be less likely to display the disruptive behaviour common in boys with autism. This could then lead to an under-diagnosis of autism in girls [16,17]. For example, the Autism Diagnostic Research Centre (ADRC) in Southampton, which specialises in diagnosing autism in adults, has received a higher than expected proportion of adult female referrals indicating that there are characteristics relating to females that may mask the early recognition of autism (ADRC Newsletter Summer 2009).

## References

1  Brugha, T S, Cooper, S A, McManus, S, Purdon, S, et al. (2012) *Estimating the prevalence of Autism Spectrum Conditions in Adults: Extending the 2007 Adult Psychiatric Morbidity Survey*, The NHS Information Centre: England.

2  Leonard, H, Dixon, G, Whitehouse, A J O, Bourke, J, et al. (2010) "Unpacking the complex nature of the autism epidemic." *Research in Autism Spectrum Disorders*, 4(4), pp. 548–554.

3  Bedford, H E and Elliman, D (2000) "Concerns about immunisation." *British Medical Journal*, 320(7229), pp. 240-243.

4  Bishop, D V M, Whitehouse, A J O, Watt, H J and Line, E A (2008) "Autism and diagnostic substitution: evidence from a study of adults with a history of developmental language disorder." *Developmental Medicine and Child Neurology*, 50(5), pp. 341–345.

5  Shattuck, P T (2006) "The contribution of diagnostic substitution to the growing administrative prevalence of autism in US special education." *Pediatrics*, 117(4), pp. 1028–1037.

6  Chakrabarti, S and Fombonne, E (2005) "Pervasive developmental disorders in preschool children: confirmation of high prevalence." *American Journal of Psychiatry*, 162(6), pp. 1133–1141.

7  Brugha, T, McManus, S, Meltzer, H, Smith, J, et al. (2009) "Autism Spectrum Disorders in adults living in households throughout England." *Report from the Adult Psychiatric Morbidity Survey 2007*.

8  Anderson, N B and Armstead, C A (1995) "Toward understanding the association of socioeconomic status and health: a new challenge for the piopsychosocial approach." *Psychosomatic Medicine*, 57(3), pp. 213–225.

9  Llaneza, D C, DeLuke, S V, Batista, M, Crawley, J N, et al. (2010) "Communication, interventions, and scientific advances in autism: a commentary." *Physiology & Behavior*, 100(3), pp. 268–276.

10  King, M and Bearman, P (2011) "Socioeconomic status and the increased prevalence of autism in California." *American Sociological Review*, 76(2), pp. 320–346.

11  Hwang, S K and Charnley, H (2010) "Honourable sacrifice: a visual ethnography of the family lives of Korean children with autistic siblings." *Children & Society*, 24(6), pp. 437–448.

12  Reiheld, A (2010) "Patient complains of … How medicalization mediates power and justice." *International Journal of Feminist Approaches to Bioethics*, 3(1), pp. 72–98.

13  Kim, Y A, Leventhal, B I, Koh, Y J, Fombonne, E, et al. (2011) "Prevalence of Autism Spectrum Disorders in a total population sample." *American Journal of Psychiatry*, 168(9), pp. 904–912.

14  Carter, C S (2007) "Sex differences in oxytocin and vasopressin: implications for autism spectrum disorders?" *Behavioural Brain Research*, 176(1), pp. 170–186.

15  Chakrabarti, B, Dudbridge, F, Kent, L, Wheelwright, S, et al. (2009) "Genes related to sex steroids, neural growth, and social-emotional behavior are associated with autistic traits, empathy, and Asperger syndrom." *Autism Research*, 2(3), pp. 157–177.

16  McLennan, J D, Lord, C and Schopler, E (1993) "Sex differences in higher functioning people with autism." *Journal of Autism and Developmental Disorders*, 23(2), pp. 217–227.

17  Gould, J and Ashton-Smith, J (2011) "Missed diagnosis or misdiagnosis? Girls and women on the autism spectrum." *GAP Journal*, 12(1), pp. 34–41.

# Chapter 4:
# Genetics of autism

Studies of twins and family members have shown that there is a strong genetic component to autism. If one identical twin has autism, the likelihood that the other twin will also have autism is at least 60%. In non-identical twins this likelihood is about 30%, while in non-twin siblings the likelihood is around 20%. A large component of autism research is dedicated to trying to find the specific genetic factors which cause autism. Some methods used by research scientists include linkage and association studies, along with mouse models. Using these methods numerous genes have been identified which are associated with autism. These include genes which are involved in the development of the nervous system as well as some involved in social interactions and sex hormones. So far, the genetic bases of 10% - 20% of cases of autism have been identified although mutations in known genes only seem to account for 1% - 2% of cases of autism. This is not really surprising when we consider the complexity and variability of autism, but it does provide challenges to scientific researchers.

It is hoped that by increasing our understanding of the genetics of autism and how the environment affects gene expression, we will eventually be able to gain a clear understanding of the development of autism at the molecular level and perhaps identify useful biomarkers to aid in diagnosis.

This chapter will introduce some general concepts in genetics and explain how advances made in this rapidly developing science are providing insights into the biological basis of autism.

The first clue that there is a strong genetic component to autism came in the 1970s with studies of twins. It was found that if a child had an identical twin with autism, the child was much more likely to also have autism than if he or she had a non-identical twin with autism[1]. Identical twins are descendant from the same zygote, the fusion of a single egg and sperm, which then splits to form two embryos (Figure 2). As a result of this identical twins carry the same genetic information and are remarkably similar in physical appearance. Non-identical, or fraternal, twins develop during the same pregnancy but are the product of two separate eggs and two separate sperm meaning that they are as genetically distinct as regular siblings.

By comparing identical and non-identical twins it was shown that the high likelihood of autism among both identical twins was not merely a consequence of having a shared environment during pregnancy. If one identical twin has autism there is at least a 60% chance that the other twin will also have autism[2-4]. Among non-identical twins, if one twin has autism there is a smaller chance that the remaining twin will have autism (about 30%[3]) and this is slightly higher than the chance that a non-twin sibling will have autism – just under 20%[2,5]. There is some additional evidence from family studies that autism is a largely genetic condition. For example, family members of people with autism often display autism-like traits that are characteristic of the broader autism phenotype such as awkwardness in communication and social interaction, to an extent that is more common than in the general population[6].

Twin and family studies showed that there is a strong genetic component to autism and were instrumental in doing away with the psychiatric theory that autism came about as a result of bad

## Figure 2

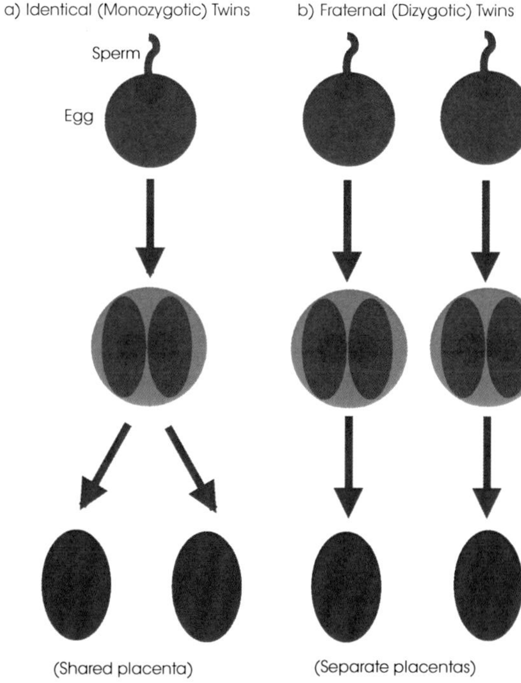

a) Identical (Monozygotic) Twins    b) Fraternal (Dizygotic) Twins

Sperm
Egg

(Shared placenta)    (Separate placentas)

parenting[7]. However, they say nothing about the precise genetic factors that are involved in determining autism such as which genes are involved and what particular mutations affecting those genes may contribute to the risk of autism. The increasing prevalence rates and the greater awareness in society of autism in recent years has led to a surge in research funding to attempt to unravel the underlying genetic basis of autism[8].

Genetics is a rapidly advancing field of research and, over the last ten years, the tools have been developed to investigate and characterise the human genome and to discover how our genes contribute to making us who we are. For the first time in history humans have the ability to identify specific genetic variations that contribute to disease susceptibility. Genetic research in recent years has led to an understanding of the causes of many inherited diseases. Elucidating the genetic causes of autism would give an insight into how autism physically manifests itself in the body as genes are ultimately the 'recipe book' for how the body develops and functions. Genetic signatures of autism could act as biomarkers of autism which could be screened for using genetic testing and this would enable the targeting of early interventions to children at the greatest risk of autism[9].

Advances in our knowledge of genetics have led to the development of a number of powerful techniques for determining the genetic basis of inherited disorders and these have been applied to the field of autism research. In simple terms finding the genes that are involved in determining a trait involves making direct associations between genetic variation and the trait of interest.

For example, if most people with autism happened to have a particular mutation in a particular gene, whereas people without autism lacked that mutation, then that would be evidence that this gene was in some way involved in determining autism. Investigating genetic variation among humans has become much easier since the human genome was characterised in 2003. The Human Genome project essentially involved determining the full sequence of nucleotide 'letters'

## Biomarkers:

An objectively measurable indicator of a biological state. Genetic biomarkers could be used for the diagnosis of autism and early diagnosis would allow earlier interventions to be carried out, improving the long term prospects for a child. The search for effective biomarkers has been one of the key aims of autism science but because autism is highly genetically and neurologically variable it has been difficult to identify biomarkers that are generally indicative of the condition.

along all 23 chromosomes, along with the relative positions of all of the genes on those chromosomes together with many of the genetic variations (due to mutations) that exist within and between the genes. This basically provided a 'map' of the genome that researchers can focus in on to investigate and determine particular regions that may be involved in determining various traits, such as genetic disorders (see "An introduction to molecular genetics" at the end of this chapter).

Although it is now clear that genes play an important role in determining autism, finding the actual genes involved is more difficult. It is now becoming clear that the genetic basis to autism is highly complex. This is perhaps unsurprising since autism affects the most complex organ in the human body - the brain - and its role in the complex behaviour of social interaction. Some diseases have a relatively simple genetic basis, such as haemophilia - where a single mutation in a single gene is generally responsible and anyone with this genetic variant will suffer from the disease[10]. In the case of autism, rather than a single gene being responsible, there appear to be multiple genes and several levels of complexity involved in determining whether people have autism[7]. It has been found that in different people different genes contribute to autism. Some gene variants appear to carry a risk for autism without directly causing it and many of these

gene variants may be required for someone to develop autism[11]. In these cases, people may inherit from their parents a genetic predisposition for autism through inheriting multiple gene variants that confer a susceptibility to autism[12].

Despite these complications much progress has been made in understanding the genetics of autism. A large number of genes contributing to the risk of autism have been identified and many of these are implicated in the development of the nervous system[13], such as in the functioning of the synapses, the junctions between nerve cells that are important for the transmission of signals across the nervous system[14]. So far, the genetic bases of 10%-20% of cases of autism have been identified, although none of the known causes accounts for more than 1%-2% of cases[11]. The discovery that there are many, perhaps even hundreds, of genes involved in determining autism is perhaps unsurprising given the large amount of variation that exists in the severity and symptoms of autism. These autism susceptibility genes are distributed throughout the genome and appear to occur on most, if not all, chromosomes[11].

There is no universal consensus yet as to the general nature of genetic changes that are involved in autism. One school of thought suggests that autism tends to result from the combined action of a number of genes that interact together[15]. All of the 'autism susceptibility' genes that have been identified carry a low individual risk for autism. Many cases of autism may occur because of interactions among different genes and when the 'right' combination of gene variants is present, autism will result. Some studies have indicated that different genes may regulate the different core domains (social, communication and repetitive/restrictive behaviours) displayed in autism[11]. There may also be interactions between genes and environmental factors, where a particular environmental stimulus may trigger the expression of autism susceptibility genes[16]. Another school of thought suggests that a large proportion of cases of autism may be due to mutations in single genes with strong effects[17]. There are some cases where if someone has a particular gene variant, they have a high likelihood of having autism, but these variants appear to be rare and have only been identified in a very small percentage of cases.

One of the most striking insights into the genetic basis of autism in the last couple of years has been the finding that copy number variations (CNVs) are important causes of autism[13]. Mutations are often thought of in terms of single nucleotide changes, where one of the nucleotide subunits of DNA is incorrectly substituted during DNA replication. However, with CNVs, large parts of genes, entire genes, or even groups of genes together can be either deleted or duplicated in the genome. Such large-scale mutations were generally thought to be rare as they were expected to have strong negative consequences for the health of affected people, so it was surprising that CNVs are actually quite common across the genome and can be present in even healthy people. There is evidence that some CNVs can actually be beneficial. For example, in cultures where there is traditionally a high consumption of starchy foods people tend to have more copies of the gene for the breakdown of starch than people in cultures that consume little starch. However, in many cases CNVs can be detrimental and are sometimes associated with pathological conditions such as in cancer formation.

In relation to autism, in a large-scale study of over 2,000 people, the Autism Genome Project consortium found that people with autism tend to have more CNVs present within their genes[18]. People without autism also had many CNVs present but these tended to be located in intergenic regions - the spaces between genes - where they were less likely to have a strong effect on the function of proteins. In people with autism, many of the CNVs were associated with the development of the central nervous system, indicating that autism results from early changes in the growth of the nervous system in embryos and infants. Beyond these general patterns, people with autism each had their own unique complement of CNVs and the most common CNV was still only present in less than 1% of people with autism. This means it was not possible to identify any single CNV that could act as a useful biomarker of autism.

Although autism is determined to a large degree by the inheritance from parents to offspring of gene variants for autism susceptibility, novel, non-inherited mutations also play a role in determining autism. Mutations can occur in a parent's sperm or egg cells, in the fertilised egg, or within cells of the early developing embryo. If this happens the child will carry mutations that are not present in either of the parents. These are known as *de novo* mutations and they may account for a substantial number of cases of autism[19]. In particular, CNVs are often *de novo* rather than inherited.

It is worth noting that in some cases autism can be secondary to a known genetic disorder with a single defined cause. Genetic disorders such as fragile X syndrome or tuberous sclerosis affect the development of the nervous system and can lead to autism as a secondary consequence as well as having other effects[20]. There are a number of these

## Genome-wide association studies:

GWAS involve taking two groups of participants: one group comprised of individuals with the disorder and a control group without the disorder. The DNA of each individual is extracted from a blood sample or cells obtained by wiping a cotton swab along the inside of the cheek and is then scanned by laboratory machines that analyse sites of known genetic variation across the genome for differences among the individuals in the study. If a particular genetic variant is found to be significantly more common in individuals with the disorder compared to the group without the disorder then it is said to be associated with the disorder and gives an indication that that particular region of the genome harbours the disorder-causing problem. It is important to note that just because a genetic variant is associated with a disorder does not mean that it is actually involved in causing the disorder itself as it may just be inherited together with the actual disorder-causing mutation. For this reason, researchers often need to take additional steps, such as sequencing DNA nucleotides in that particular region of the genome, to identify the exact genetic change involved in the disease[23].

established genetic disorders although they are individually very rare and together account for only about 10% of cases of autism[21]. Also, none of the genetic disorders are specific to autism because each of them includes both people with and without autism. A number of powerful molecular biology techniques

**Linkage mapping:**
This approach is similar to association studies in the sense that it looks for associations between autism traits and genetic variation across the genome. However, while association studies deal with unrelated individuals, linkage mapping analyses the inheritance patterns of traits within families and how traits are transmitted from one generation to the next. This approach typically investigates many families, with large numbers of parents and offspring, and attempts to find genetic variants that are 'linked' (inherited alongside) to the traits of interest. The general principle is that the closer a genetic variant is physically on a chromosome to the gene that is determining the trait of interest, the more often they will be inherited together. This approach can be used to narrow down the region of the genome where the causative gene is likely to be located.

have been used to identify the genetic basis of autism. One recent large Genome-wide association study (GWAS) investigated the genomes of thousands of people with and without autism[22]. Over half a million sites in the genome where genetic variation is known to occur were investigated in both groups and six sites were found to be significantly more common in people with autism. All of the sites associated with autism were located close together in the same region of the genome and lay in the region between two genes called *CDH9* and *CDH10*. These two genes produce proteins that are important for the production of synapses and are critical for the normal development of neurons. Mutations that affect these genes may cause problems with the development of connections in the brain which could lead to autism.

One of the weaknesses of GWAS is that they are generally restricted to analysing sites of the genome that are already known to harbour common genetic variants and do not consider sites where rare mutations may occur. This means that if autism is caused more by rare mutations of strong effect, association studies will not be of much use for discovering these. One way to overcome this problem would be to sequence the entire genome of people with and without autism so that every single variable site within the genome, whether common or rare, could be investigated for associations with autism. This may be possible within a few years, although at present it is too expensive to be carried out.

Another powerful technique that has been used in genetic research into autism is called linkage mapping. One success of linkage studies was the identification of the gene *CNTNAP2* (also know as the 'cat-nap' gene) as contributing to the risk of autism[24]. *CNTNAP2* is involved in brain development and is expressed in the frontal and temporal lobes, which are known to develop differently in people with autism. Having a risk variant of *CNTNAP2* does not automatically result in autism but it may affect development in a subtle way that increases the risk of autism in conjunction with other genetic or environmental factors.

Although linkage and association studies have identified genes in a number of chromosomal regions that may be involved in autism, it has proven difficult to replicate these results[13]. This is perhaps unsurprising considering the complexity and variability of autism and the fact that most genes only contribute a small risk for autism individually. Typically, using larger numbers of patients in a study will result in greater power to detect genetic variants associated with autism. Larger-scale investigations in the future, along with improved methods of analysis, should enable GWAS and linkage studies to pinpoint rarer genetic variants associated with autism with greater accuracy.

Genetic studies have identified many risk variants for autism, but approaches such as linkage analysis and GWAS are limited in that they do not show whether a particular genetic variant actually causes autism. For example, some genetic variants may be risk

## Animal models:

This approach involves producing a strain of transgenic, or 'mutant', animals which carry a particular mutant gene that has been previously identified in humans. In autism research, laboratory mice are commonly used since these animals are easy to keep and breed but also have complex social behaviours that can be observed and studied. Using techniques of molecular biology, genes can be introduced, deleted, or modified within the genomes of mouse embryos which are then allowed to develop to adulthood. In this way, mice with suspected 'autism genes' can be produced and these are subjected to tests of social interactions to compare their behavioural traits with normal mice that do not have the 'autism gene'. If the mutant mice display autism-like behaviour, this is evidence for a causal role for the gene variant in determining autism.

factors because they tend to be inherited together with a gene that causes autism rather than having a causative role themselves. One way to determine whether a gene is directly involved in causing autism is to use an animal model system. For example, a mouse model deficient for the *Pten* gene, which is implicated in autism through a screening of people with autism, displayed problems with learning and memory[25]. Another strain of mice was created to be deficient for *Shank3*, a gene that is involved in the transmission of neural signals. These display autism-like traits, such as avoiding contact with other mice and engaging in repetitive behaviours like self-injurious grooming[26]. Defective copies of the *SHANK3* gene are highly associated with autism in humans, although it is responsible for less than 1% of cases overall.

The identification of genes that are involved in autism and understanding how they interact and affect the structure and function of the brain will be important for gaining insights into what the specific causes of autism are and aid in the development of better diagnostic procedures and treatments for affected people. Also, by understanding the genetic factors of autism it may be possible to classify autism in stricter and more biologically meaningful subtypes. If the genetic basis of autism was better understood, it would be possible to investigate the potential interactions between genes and the environment that may lead to autism. This could help in the identification of possible environmental factors that may be involved.

Despite the powerful modern genetic techniques available to researchers there are a number of obstacles to gaining a full understanding of the genetic basis of autism. It is possible that what is classed under the umbrella of autism may in fact be a number of distinct conditions, each with different underlying genetic causes. If this is the case, then by grouping the distinct conditions together it will be difficult to find strong genetic determinants that underlie each of them separately. With the development of more sophisticated diagnostic tools it may become possible to separate patients into distinct sub-categories of autism which could then be considered separately in different genetic studies.

The many different genes that appear to be involved in autism along with the nature of the mutations that can affect these genes, such as being inherited or de novo, rare or common, seems to indicate that there can be multiple paths to autism. It is possible that the different genes involved may have common functional characteristics, particularly in relation to the development of the nervous system. For example, mutations in different genes may have common consequences for the development of the brain and could lead to the same end result of autism. In fact, many of the genes that have been associated with risk of autism seem to cluster into relatively few functional roles, such as cell growth and proliferation, as well as cell-cell communication. In order to fully understand the physical changes that take place in the brains of people with autism it is necessary to study the brain itself, and this is the focus of the next chapter.

## Summary points

- Studies of twins and family members show that autism has a strong genetic component.
- Modern genetic methods allow scientists to search for the specific genetic factors causing autism.
- Linkage and association studies, along with mouse models, have led to the identification of numerous genes associated with autism.
- These include genes involved in nervous system development, social interactions and sex hormones.
- Copy number variations in genes are commonly associated with autism.

# Focus on: An introduction to molecular genetics

In order to understand the approaches that researchers have used in attempting to determine the genetic basis of autism, it is necessary to have an understanding of what genes are and how they work. A gene is essentially a stretch of DNA that contains the information necessary for the production of a biological product, in most cases a protein. DNA is comprised of a large molecule of repeating subunits which are held together by chemical bonds. Although there are only four different types of DNA subunits (known in abbreviation as A, T, C and G, or collectively as nucleotides), these can occur in many different possible combinations along a DNA strand, and strings of several hundred or thousands of these subunits comprise the genes that provide the information necessary for each protein. There are often large regions of DNA located between genes that do not have any direct role in protein production. These 'intergenic' regions actually make up over 90% of the total DNA (or genome) of humans and the actual functions of this DNA have not been fully worked out yet.

Proteins are molecules that either drive the many chemical reactions that take place in the body, or have important structural and mechanical roles, such as providing the materials that make up tendons, hair and nails. As such, proteins are vital for the proper functioning and maintenance of health in the body. This means that when mutations occur in genes that disrupt the functions of proteins, these can have major consequences for the health of an individual. Mutations are errors that affect the nucleotide sequence of DNA and usually occur during the replication of DNA, which happens every time a cell divides. DNA replication is a complex process that involves the interaction of a number of different enzymes and other components and it is not uncommon for errors to occur in the functioning of this biological apparatus, such as addition of the wrong nucleotide to the replicating strand or incorrect copying or deletion of stretches of DNA. Different types of mutations can occur. Some mutations result in the changing of a single nucleotide and are called single nucleotide polymorphisms (SNPs). Other mutations involve the duplication or deletion of entire sections of DNA and are called copy number variations (CNVs). The extent of the damage that mutations cause depends on the precise changes that result and where they occur. Mutations that prevent proteins being correctly produced can often be lethal, whereas mutations that occur in intergenic regions are often harmless since they do not directly affect protein production. Most mutations actually occur within intergenic regions and do not appear to negatively affect health or survival either way. This means that there is quite a bit of genetic variability among people due to harmless mutations that have appeared in the genome over time and been passed down through generations.

There are about 20,000 genes in the human genome and these are arranged into 23 long coiled strands of DNA called chromosomes. Almost every cell in the body contains two sets of these 23 chromosomes and one set is inherited from each of our parents. For 22 of the chromosome pairs, each of the chromosomes of the pair carries the same complement of genes. The final pair are called the sex chromosomes and are designated as either X or Y. Females have two copies of the X chromosome whereas males have an X and a Y chromosome. Because each cell in the body contains the same complement of genes, it is possible to extract a DNA sample from our saliva (which contains cells from the lining of the mouth) and use this to gain information about genes that may only function in other parts of the body, such as the liver or brain. However, although the same genes are present in each cell, only certain groups of genes will be activated, or 'expressed', among different tissue types. This tissue-specific gene expression is what makes different tissue types distinguishable from one another.

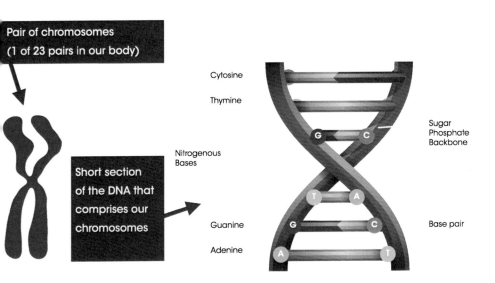

**Pair of chromosomes (1 of 23 pairs in our body)**

Short section of the DNA that comprises our chromosomes

Cytosine

Thymine

Nitrogenous Bases

Guanine

Adenine

Sugar Phosphate Backbone

Base pair

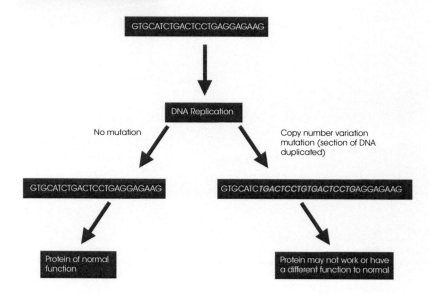

Effect of a mutation in a DNA region necessary for protein function

GTGCATCTGACTCCTGAGGAGAAG

DNA Replication

No mutation

Copy number variation mutation (section of DNA duplicated)

GTGCATCTGACTCCTGAGGAGAAG

GTGCATC*TGACTCCTGTGACTCCTG*AGGAGAAG

Protein of normal function

Protein may not work or have a different function to normal

## References

1 Folstein, S and Rutter, M (1977) "Infantile autism: a genetic study of 21 twin pairs." *The Journal of Child Psychology and Psychiatry*, 18(4), pp. 297–321.

2 Folstein, S and Rosen-Sheidley, B (2001) "Genetics of autism: complex aetiology for a heterogeneous disorder." *Nature Reviews Genetics*, 2(12), pp. 943–955.

3 Hallmayer, J, Cleveland, S, Torres, A, Phillips, J, et al. (2011) "Genetic heritability and shared environmental factors among twin pairs with autism." *Archives of general psychiatry*, 68(11), pp. 1095–102.

4 Muhle, R, Trentacoste, S V and Rapin, I (2004) "The genetics of autism." *Pediatrics*, 113(5), pp. e472–e486.

5  Ozonoff, S, Young, G S, Carter, A, Messinger, D, et al. (2011) "Recurrence risk for autism spectrum disorders: a Baby Siblings Research Consortium study." *Pediatrics*, 128(3), pp. e488–95.

6  Piven, J, Palmer, P, Jacobi, D, Childress, D and Arndt, S (1997) "Broader autism phenotype: evidence from a family history study of multiple-incidence autism families." *American Journal of Psychiatry*, 154(2), pp. 185–190.

7  Geschwind, D H (2009) "Advances in autism." *Annual Review of Medicine*, 60, pp. 367–380.

8  Singh, J, Illes, J, Lazzeroni, L and Hallmayer, J (2009) "Trends in US autism research funding." *Journal of Autism and Developmental Disorders*, 39(5), pp. 788–795.

9  Herbert, M R, Russo, J P, Yang, S, Roohi, J, et al. (2006) "Autism and environmental genomics." *Neurotoxicology*, 27(5), pp. 671–684.

10  Graw, J, Brachmann, H H, Oldenburg, J, Schneppenheim, R, et al. (2005) "Haemophilia A: from mutation analysis to new therapies." *Nature Reviews Genetics*, 6(6), pp. 488–501.

11  Abrahams, B S and Geschwind, D H (2008) "Advances in autism genetics: on the threshold of a new neurobiology." *Nature Reviews Genetics*, 9(5), pp. 341–355.

12  Skuse, D H (2007) "Rethinking the nature of genetic vulnerability to autistic spectrum disorders." *Trends in Genetics*, 23(8), pp. 387–395.

13  Glessner, J T, Wang, K, Cai, G, Korvatska, O, et al. (2009) "Autism genome-wide copy number variation reveals ubiquitin and neuronal genes." *Nature*, 459(7246), pp. 569–575.

14  Persico, A M (2006) "Searching for ways out of the autism maze: genetic, epigenetic and environmental clues." *Trends in Neurosciences*, 29(7), pp. 349–358.

15  Nishimura, Y, Martin, C L, Vazquez-Lopez, A, Spence, S J, et al. (2007) "Genome-wide expression profiling of lymphoblastoid cell lines distinguishes different forms of autism and reveals shared pathways." *Human Molecular Genetics*, 16(14), pp. 1682–1698.

16  Deth, R, Muratore, C, Benzecry, J, Power-Charnitsky, V A and Waly, M (2008) "How environmental and genetic factors combine to cause autism: a redox/methylation hypothesis." *Neurotoxicology*, 29(1), pp. 190–201.

17  Geschwind, D H (2008) "Autism: many genes, common pathways?" *Cell*, 135(3), pp. 391–395.

18  Szatmari, P, Paterson, A D, Zaigenbaum, L, Roberts, W, et al. (2007) "Mapping autism risk loci using genetic linkage and chromosomal rearrangements." *Nature Genetics*, 39(3), pp. 319–329.

19  Beaudet, A L (2007) "Autism: highly heritable but not inherited." *Nature Medecine*, 13(5), pp. 534–536.

20  Cohen, D, Pichard, N, Tordjman, S, Baumann, C, et al. (2005) "Specific genetic disorders and autism: clinical contribution towards their identification." *Journal of Autism and Developmental Disorders*, 35(1), pp. 103–116.

21  Marshall, C R, Noor, A, Vincent, J B, Lionel, A C, et al. (2008) "Structural variation of chromosomes in autism spectrum disorder." *American Journal of Human Genetics*, 82(2), pp. 477–488.

22  Wang, K, Zhang, H, Ma, D, Bucan, M, et al. (2009) "Common genetic variants on 5p14.1 associate with autism spectrum disorders." *Nature*, 459(7246), pp. 528–533.

23  NIH (2011) "Genome-Wide Association Studies." [Online] Available from: http://www.genome.gov/20019523 (Accessed 11 March 2013)

24  Arking, D E, Cutler, D J, Brune, C W, Teslovich, T M, et al. (2008) "A common genetic variant in the neurecin superfamily member CNTNAP2 increases familial risk of autism." *American Journal of Human Genetics*, 82(1), pp. 160–164.

25  Kwon, C H, Luikart, B W, Powell, C M, Zhou, J, et al. (2006) "Pten regulates neuronal arborization and social interaction in mice." *Neuron*, 50(3), pp. 377–388.

26  Peca, J, Feliciano, C, Ting, J T, Wang, W, et al. (2011) "Shank3 mutant mice display autistic-like behaviours and striatal dysfunction." *Nature*, 472(7344), pp. 437–442.

# Chapter 5:
# Neurobiology of autism

Brain imaging techniques and post-mortem studies have provided us with some insight into how the nervous systems of people with autism develop. Although there is a lot of developmental variability among people with autism, a number of patterns have emerged. The brains of people with autism seem to undergo accelerated growth in early development. For example, some regions of the brain involved in social interactions seem to undergo initial increased growth which is then followed by a decrease in the number of neurons present in that brain region. Changes may also occur in how certain parts of the brain are connected to each other. Furthermore, the way that certain genes are expressed in the brain seems to be different in people with autism, indicating the crucial role that genetics plays in how the brain develops differently in these individuals.

This chapter will highlight some of the exciting research that has been recently conducted in the field of neurobiology and the contribution this has made to our understanding of autism.

A number of modern brain imaging techniques, such as magnetic resonance imaging (MRI) and positron emission tomography (PET) have been used to unravel the neural systems affected by autism. These approaches have provided a wide range of findings about how the brains of people with autism develop. Just as with the results of genetic research, there has been a great deal of variation identified in autism brain structure and function[1], and the patterns found from brain studies do not apply to all people with autism.

Many brain imaging studies have used small sample sizes and the methodologies used among studies often vary, making them difficult to compare to one another. Some recent studies have shown that the artefacts caused by head movement during an MRI scan can look very similar to the patterns seen in people with autism, which casts doubt on some studies and highlights the need for new techniques to reduce the effects of head movement[2]. However, some imaging studies have been replicated and there are some trends in autism brain development emerging[1]

## Brain imaging:

These approaches are used to non-invasively construct a three-dimensional image of the structure or metabolic processes of the body, based on the physical properties of different tissues. For **magnetic resonance imaging (MRI)**, the patient lies inside a large tube containing a series of strong magnets. A magnetic field is switched on that aligns the protons in the body similar to the needle on a compass. A pulse of radio waves is then emitted that causes the protons to be knocked out of alignment and each proton emits a signal that can be used to identify its location. These signals are detected by a scanning instrument which uses the information to construct a detailed three-dimensional image of the interior of the brain. **Positron emission tomography (PET)** scans involve injecting a radioactive version of a natural chemical, such as glucose or water, into the body. This chemical then travels to the sites of the body where it is normally used in biological processes and emits particles called positrons, which are detected by an instrument and used to create an image. This provides information about the activity and function of different parts of the brain.

The brains of children with autism often have different structural features compared to children without autism[3]. To investigate this, one MRI study took measurements of the brains of children with autism at 2 years old and again at 4 or 5 years old to determine how they developed over time[4]. It was found that although certain parts of the brain were larger in children with autism than those without, the rates of growth were similar over the period of the study. This indicates that the period of accelerated brain growth occurs early on in development, before 2 years of age. It also occurs before the actual symptoms of autism appear. Understanding the patterns of brain growth in children with autism could potentially provide diagnostic markers allowing the early intervention of therapeutic treatments. Unfortunately, performing brain imaging on very young children is both expensive and technically difficult, making this field of enquiry challenging.

It also appears that, in autism, there are certain regions of the brain that undergo more exaggerated growth than other areas of the brain. The frontal and temporal lobes of the cerebral cortex, the area responsible for higher-order functions such as abstract reasoning, have been found to have particularly increased growth in children with autism[5]. The frontal lobe is involved in creativity, emotion and speech and the temporal lobe is involved in hearing and language. The amygdala, a region located within the temporal lobe, is important for the regulation of emotion and social interactions and often has increased growth in children with autism[6]. Using post-mortem brain tissue taken from subjects 10 - 44 years old, researchers did not find any difference in the size of the amygdala among people with or without autism but they did find that autism was associated with a reduction in the numbers of neurons (nerve cells) present[7]. It also appears that the amygdala undergoes an abnormal growth trajectory in autism with an initial period of increased growth followed by a reduction in the number of neurons.

Although imaging techniques have been very useful for the study of neurodevelopmental changes in the brain, they are limited with respect to investigating very fine-scale patterns of structure and development. Post-mortem studies allow for the micro-structural analysis of tissues and have been performed on the brains of people with autism to identify changes in the nervous system, such as abnormal patterns of neuron growth and migration and altered development of synapses. However, there have been very few post-mortem studies performed to date and they typically involve older subjects who are likely to display additional changes to their brains unrelated to the development of autism[8].

In autism research, it is important to reconcile the findings from direct studies of the brain with those of genetics in order to build up a more complete picture of its biological basis. Brain imaging and post-mortem studies can be useful for informing genetic approaches and vice versa. There are several studies that have shown direct associations between particular genes and autism brain development. For example, there is a particular variant of the *CNTNAP2* gene (discussed in Chapter 4) that carries a high risk for autism and is expressed most highly in the frontal lobe, consistent with a possible role in abnormal development of this region. One MRI study found that children with the risk variant of *CNTNAP2* had abnormally developed brains with reduced connectivity and lack of long-range connections to other regions of the brain[9].

Other studies have used post-mortem brain tissue to investigate the patterns of gene expression displayed in the brains of people with autism. One study that performed this found that there were over 400 genes expressed differently in the cerebral cortex samples from an autism group compared to controls, but not in other areas such as the cerebellum[10]. Within the cerebral cortex, in neurotypical brains, there were several hundred genes expressed differently between the frontal and temporal lobes,

whereas in the brains of people with autism there were fewer differences between these two regions. In this sense, the frontal and temporal lobes of patients with autism were similar and the features that normally distinguish the two regions were less evident. Many of the genes that were under-expressed in brains of people with autism were known to be involved in the formation of synapses, and mutant variants in these genes had been previously been associated with autism.

A picture that is emerging is that autism may be the result of a disruption to networks of genes involved in the development of neurons. Many different genes comprise these networks, and the correct functioning of most if not all of them is required for normal brain development. This means that there are lots of possibilities for the developmental

## Gene expression:

Thousands of genes are expressed, or 'switched-on', in a living tissue at any one time. These patterns reflect the production and activities of the proteins present. As such, gene expression patterns are important regulators of the development of the nervous system. When a gene is expressed it produces an intermediate product called RNA, which leads on to the production of a protein. It is possible to extract the RNA from tissues and perform analyses to determine the patterns of gene expression present.

process to be thrown off course by mutations. There is a lot of variation among the brains of people with autism and if a number of randomly selected people with autism are screened, they are likely to all have different causative mutations and slightly different patterns of brain development. However, it is starting to become clear that there are particular commonalities of genetic pathways and brain development involved in autism and that these are related to each other.

## Summary points

- The development of the brain in autism has been investigated using brain imaging and post-mortem studies.
- There is a lot of variability present but some patterns have emerged.
- In autism, the brain often undergoes accelerated growth in early development.
- Regions of the brain involved in social interactions undergo initial increased growth, followed by reductions in the number of neurons present.
- Connections between certain parts of the brain may be reduced in people with autism.
- Patterns of gene expression are also altered in people with autism.

**References**

1  Geschwind, D H (2009) "Advances in autism." *Annual Review of Medicine*, 60, pp. 367–380.

2  Deen, B and Pelphrey, K (2012) "Perspective: Brain scans need a rethink." *Nature*, 491(7422), p. S20.

3  Fombonne, E, Roge, B, Claverie, J, Courty, S and Fremolle, J (1999) "Microcephaly and macrocephaly in autism." *Journal of Autism and Developmental Disorders*, 29(2), pp. 113–119.

4  Hazlett, H C, Poe, M D, Gerig, G, Styner, M, et al. (2011) "Early brain overgrowth in autism associated with an increase in cortical surface area before age 2 years." *Archives of General Psychiatry*, 68(5), pp. 467–476.

5  Courchesne, E, Pierce, K, Schumann, C M, Redcay, E, et al. (2007) "Mapping early brain development in autism." *Neuron*, 56(2), pp. 399–413.

6  Schumann, C M, Hamstra, J, Goodlin-Jones, B L, Lotspeich, L J, et al. (2004) "The amygdala is enlarged in children but not adolescents with autism; the hippocampus is enlarged at all ages." *Neurobiology of Disease*, 24(28), pp. 6392–6401.

7  Schumann, C M and Amaral, D G (2006) "Stereological analysis of amygdala neuron number in autism." *The Journal of Neuroscience*, 26(29), pp. 7674–7679.

8  Persico, A M (2006) "Searching for ways out of the autism maze: genetic, epigenetic and environmental clues." *Trends in Neurosciences*, 29(7), pp. 349–358.

9  Scott-Van Zeeland, A A, Abrahams, B S, Alvarez-Retuerto, A I, Sonnenblick, L I, et al. (2010) "Altered functional connectivity in frontal lobe circuits is associated with variation in the autism risk gene CNTNAP2." *Science Translational Medicine*, 2(56), p. 56ra80.

10  Voineagu, I, Wang, X, Johnston, P, Lowe, J K, et al. (2011) "Transcriptomatic analysis of autistic brain reveals convergent molecular pathology." *Nature*, 474(7351), pp. 380–384.

# Chapter 6:
# Environmental factors and autism

Many environmental factors could potentially contribute to autism risk. However, few have so far been identified. To address this issue, a number of large epidemiological studies are currently underway to attempt to identify relationships between autism and the environment. These studies have highlighted the possibility that timing of conception and whether or not prenatal vitamin supplements are taken may be associated with autism. There are also some known environmental risk factors for autism such as exposure to thalidomide or valproic acid during pregnancy or whether the mother suffers from rubella during pregnancy. Finally there is growing evidence that interactions between genes and the environment may play a role in autism.

This chapter will explore the research that is being conducted into the environmental factors which may trigger of autism and how this is shaping our understanding of the relationship between autism and the environment.

Although it is now clear that genetics play a major role in determining autism, it is likely that there is also some environmental component involved. This is because there are cases of genetically identical twins where one twin has autism and the other twin does not. Additionally, even though a large component of the dramatic rise in autism prevalence can be explained by changes in diagnostic practices (see Chapter 3), there has been speculation that some of the rise may be due to changing environmental conditions[1]. It is likely that there are a wide range of environmental factors that could potentially contribute to autism risk, from agrichemicals and pharmaceuticals to lifestyle and nutritional choices. However, merely establishing a correlation between an environmental variable and increased prevalence of autism is insufficient to show a causal relationship between them.

A wide range of environmental factors have been proposed as triggers of autism but the majority of these are highly speculative, without any strong empirical basis. In particular, most attention has focused on the possible role of various types of vaccine, in particular MMR and vaccines containing the preservative thimerosal[2]. As explained later, there have been multiple, large-scale epidemiological studies that have provided conclusive evidence against a role for vaccines in causing autism. However, the search for environmental contributors to autism has not progressed far and there is currently a huge gap in our understanding of the environmental factors which may trigger autism.

Until recently, there was relatively little research undertaken in this area, with most attention being focussed on understanding the genetic basis of autism. In the last few years there have been a number of large epidemiological studies initiated to address the relationship between autism and the environment. The Norwegian Mother and Child Cohort Study (MoBa) is a massive survey of mothers and babies, with huge amounts of data still being analysed. It will provide materials to indicate possible environmental factors associated with autism but studies are still in progress.

Another is the CHARGE (Childhood Autism Risks from Genetics and the Environment) project established at the University of California-Davis Center[3]. This project investigates numerous potential environmental risk factors for autism including factors that affect brain development, chemicals in the environment, medical history and diet. For example, one study compared the maternal intake of prenatal vitamins around the time of conception between a group of children with autism and a group with normal development. It was found that mothers that did not take prenatal vitamins were more likely to have a child with autism and that particular genetic variants associated with autism greatly increased this risk[4]. Prenatal vitamins have high concentrations of B vitamins and folic acid that are known to be important in neurodevelopment[5] and this study suggested a beneficial role for prenatal vitamins in reducing the risk of autism. It also supported the idea that autism is triggered prior to birth rather than around the time when the symptoms become manifest and demonstrated an interaction between genetic factors and the environmental factor of vitamin intake.

Another recent epidemiological study investigated associations between the time of year of conception and autism risk[6]. It found that children conceived during winter months had a significantly higher risk of autism than those conceived during the summer, although the effect was relatively small. This indicated that certain environmental factors that contribute to autism, perhaps relating to the risk of catching an infectious disease, may be more prevalent during the winter. An alternative speculation is that winter conceptions may tend to result from couples whose levels of nourishment, such as vitamin intake, are poorer than in the summer months.
Another possible connection between

autism and the environment is in relation to levels of testosterone in the womb during pregnancy. Boys are four times more likely than girls to be diagnosed with autism and it has been proposed that an excess of foetal testosterone may contribute to the development of autism[7].

It has been proposed that certain genetic variants may predispose a person to autism but that environmental triggers are then necessary to develop the condition. People with the predisposition may be particularly susceptible to environmental factors that would not affect the rest of the population. Although a diagnosis of autism is usually made around 3 or 4 years of age, the events that trigger the onset of autism could occur much earlier. Complex interactions are known to take place between genes and the environment in relation to other traits. For example, the patterns of gene expression in different tissues can vary dramatically depending on the environment. These interactions can be very difficult to unravel and the search for environmental causes of autism has so far not produced many tangible results.

One possible way that interactions can occur between the environment and genetic susceptibilities is through epigenetics. Epigenetics refers to changes in the way that genes are regulated that do not depend on changes to the actual DNA sequence of the gene. These can include environmentally induced chemical factors that bind to DNA and prevent its expression. Through epigenetic mechanisms aspects of the environment may influence how the genetic code is read and this could have consequences for the development of autism. Research into the epigenetic basis of autism is at an early stage although preliminary evidence suggests that epigenetic factors do play a role in autism susceptibility[8].

There are a small number of cases where clear associations have been made between environmental factors and increased risk of autism. Prenatal exposure to the rubella virus leads to a strong increase in the risk of autism and there have been a small number of cases reported of autism developing following maternal infection with other viruses such as cytomegalovirus and herpes[9]. Furthermore, there is growing evidence that some cases of autism could have occurred as a result of an immune response in the mother[10-12]. Early in utero exposure to thalidomide and valproic acid is also associated with autism[13]. Even taken together, these exposures are rare and unlikely to make a significant contribution to the number of cases of autism. However, these cases do support the idea that exposure to particular environmental agents during critical periods of development could lead to autism.

One possible connection between autism and the environment that has received substantial interest is that increasing parental age is associated with an increase in likelihood of offspring having autism[14]. This may be because people who fit into the 'broader autism phenotype' - that is, people who have certain mild autism-like traits below the level of a diagnosis - may tend to marry and have children at a later age. Their children, through inheriting their parents' autism susceptibility genes, may also have a greater likelihood of developing autism. An alternative explanation is that older sperm may be more likely to have acquired *de novo* mutations that increase the risk of autism[15]. Recent work seems to show that there is an increased risk of autism if the parents are older[14,16-18] but further research is needed to fully understand how the age of parents contributes to the risk of autism. However, if there is a modern trend towards people having children later in life, this may contribute to an increase in autism prevalence.

There are probably multiple environmental factors that interact with multiple genetic variants to result in the wide array of autism traits that occur. The development of large epidemiological studies such as the MoBa study and the CHARGE project coupled with improvements in our understanding of genetic risk factors for autism will enable data to be collected from thousands of people which can be used to determine associations between autism, genes and the environment. This will hopefully lead to an insight into the environmental factors contributing to autism.

## Summary points

- Many potential environmental factors could contribute to autism risk but few have been identified.
- A number of large epidemiological studies are addressing the relationship between autism and the environment.
- Timing of conception and prenatal vitamin supplementation are associated with autism.
- Known environmental risk factors for autism include thalidomide, valproic acid and prenatal rubella.
- Epigenetic interaction between genes and the environment may play a role in autism.

**References**

1 London, E and Etzel, R A (2000) "The environment as an etiologic factor in autism: a new direction for research." *Environmental Health Perspectives*, 108(Suppl 3), pp. 401–404.

2 Gerber, J S and Offit, P A (2009) "Vaccines and autism: a tale of shifting hypotheses." *Clinical Infectious Diseases*, 48(4), pp. 456–461.

3 Hertz-Picciotto, I, Croen, L A, Hansen, R, Jones, C R, et al. (2006) "The CHARGE study: an epidemiologic investigation of genetic and environmental factors contributing to autism." *Environmental Health Perspectives*, 114(7), pp. 1119–1125.

4 Schmidt, R J, Hansen, R, Hartiala, J, Allayee, H, et al. (2011) "Prenatal vitamins, one-carbon metabolism gene variants, and risk for autism." *Epidemiology*, 22(4), pp. 476–485.

5  Czeizel, A E and Dudas, I (1992) "Prevention of the first occurrence of neural-tube defects by periconceptional vitamin supplementation." *New England Journal of Medicine*, 327(26), pp. 1832–1835.

6  Zerbo, O, Iosif, A M, Delwiche, L, Walkerm, C and Hertz-Picciotto, I (2011) "Month of conception and risk of autism." *Epidemology*, 22(4), pp. 469–475.

7  Baron-Cohen, S, Lombardo, M V, Auyeung, B, Ashwin, E, et al. (2011) "Why are Autism Spectrum Conditions more prevalent in males?" *PloS Biology*, 9(6), p. e1001081.

8  Schanen, N C (2006) "Epigenetics of autism spectrum disorders." *Human Molecular Genetics*, 15(Spec No. 2), pp. R138–R150.

9  Folstein, S and Rosen-Sheidley, B (2001) "Genetics of autism: complex aetiology for a heterogeneous disorder." *Nature Reviews Genetics*, 2(12), pp. 943–955.

10  Braunschweig, D, Duncanson, P, Boyce, R, Hansen, R, et al. (2012) "Behavioral correlates of maternal antibody status among children with autism." *Journal of autism and developmental disorders*, 42(7), pp. 1435–45.

11  Heuer, L, Braunschweig, D, Ashwood, P, Van de Water, J and Campbell, D B (2011) "Association of a MET genetic variant with autism-associated maternal autoantibodies to fetal brain proteins and cytokine expression." *Translational psychiatry*, 1(10), p. e48.

12  Ziats, M N and Rennert, O M (2011) "Expression profiling of autism candidate genes during human brain development implicates central immune signaling pathways." *PloS one*, 6(9), p. e24691.

13  Bromley, R L, Mawer, G, Calyton-Smith, J and Baker, G A (2008) "Autism spectrum disorders following in utero exposure to antiepileptic drugs." *Neurology*, 71(23), pp. 1923–1924.

14  Shelton, J F, Tancredi, D J and Hertz-Picciotto, I (2010) "Independent and dependent contributions of advanced maternal and paternal ages to autism risk." *Autism Research*, 3(1), pp. 30–39.

15  Reichenberg, A, Gross, R, Weiser, M, Bresnahan, M, et al. (2006) "Advancing paternal age and autism." *Archives of General Psychiatry*, 63(9), pp. 1026–1032.

16  Buizer-Voskamp, JE, Laan, W, Staal, W G, Hennekam, E A M, et al. (2011) "Paternal age and psychiatric disorders: findings from a Dutch population registry." *Schizophrenia Research*, 129(2-3), pp. 128–132. [online] Available from: http://www.sciencedirect.com/science/article/pii/S0920996411001691 (Accessed 15 February 2013)

17  Grether, J K, Anderson, M C, Croen, L A, Smith, D and Windham, G C (2009) "Risk of autism and increasing maternal and paternal age in a large north American population." *American journal of epidemiology*, 170(9), pp. 1118–26. [online] Available from: http://www.ncbi.nlm.nih.gov/pubmed/19783586 (Accessed 15 February 2013)

18  Van Balkom, I D C, Bresnahan, M, Vuijk, P J, Hubert, J, et al. (2012) "Paternal age and risk of autism in an ethnically diverse, non-industrialized setting: Aruba." *PloS one*, 7(9), p. e45090.

# Chapter 7:
# Improving the lives of people with autism

A number of interventions for autism have been developed. These are not designed to cure autism but instead to help people with autism become better adjusted to their environments, increase their social skills and improve their quality of life. Applied Behavioural Analysis is used to reinforce desirable behaviours and discourage undesirable ones. The TEACCH educational system was developed to take into account differences in how children with autism perceive the world. Augmentative and Alternative Communication is designed to enable people with severe language difficulties to communicate via other means. There are also some biomedical interventions which tend to be used to treat psychiatric symptoms which can be associated with autism, rather than autism itself. It is important to bear in mind that because everyone with autism is different some interventions which have been shown to be effective for some people may not be effective in others.

This chapter will consider the various available interventions for autism and how these can lead to improvements in social skills and quality of life.

Although there is no cure for autism there are a number of interventions available which can help people with autism become better adjusted to their environments. In light of the many available interventions that are claimed to be effective for autism, parents need to be very discerning about which ones to select. One of the key questions to ask regarding an intervention is - is it effective? The only way to accurately assess this is to be aware of what evidence there is to back up the claims that are made regarding different interventions. Scientific investigations use well defined, measurable criteria to test hypotheses through careful experimentation. Rather than accepting claims out of hand, science involves the collection of objective data to support or contradict a theory and keeps these data separate from speculations and opinion. In this way, reliable evidence can be accumulated regarding the validity of various interventions.

The purpose of research into effective interventions for people with autism is to enable applications that will enhance their development and improve their quality of life. People with autism can learn and develop and there are some effective interventions that can help them to gain skills and improve their quality of life. Indeed, the evidence suggests that early interventions are beneficial for the development of children with autism and can lead to more positive behaviours[1,2].

The most widely used autism interventions are psychological and educational in nature[3]. Applied Behavioural Analysis (ABA) involves reinforcing particular desirable behaviours and discouraging undesirable ones. There are a number of different approaches that can be used in ABA which vary in terms of how structured they are and their emphasis on play activities. Many peer-reviewed scientific studies using both single subject study designs and group designs have demonstrated that ABA can be an effective intervention for autism[4-8]. There is evidence that ABA can be particularly effective when it is strongly implemented at a young age[2,7,9].

One educational system that has been widely used for the treatment of autism is The Treatment and Education of Autistic and Related Communication Handicapped Children (TEACCH). This intervention began in 1966 and is designed to take account of differences in how people with autism perceive the world. For example there is often an emphasis on learning through visual instruction, as visual skills in people with autism tend to be better than verbal skills. The teaching sessions are designed to be highly structured and predictable in order to take into account the difficulties that people with autism have in dealing with novel and spontaneous situations.

TEACCH programs are popular and implemented around the world and are widely regarded as potentially being effective for improving social skills and communication, as well as quality of life, for people with autism[3]. Despite its popularity, relatively few scientific studies have been performed to objectively investigate the validity of TEACCH, although a few small studies have provided evidence of effectiveness[10,11]. Until larger-scale studies are performed, TEACCH remains a promising but relatively untested intervention for autism.

Augmentative and Alternative Communication (AAC) methods are designed to help people with severe speech and language difficulties to be able to communicate using different means, with the aim of improving their ability to communicate and to develop language skills[12]. AAC systems include using sign language, gestures or the Picture Exchange Communication System (PECS) which involves communicating by pointing at picture cards. These methods can be effective for improving speech when they are taught using ABA and are suitable interventions for children with severe communication difficulties, although overall their benefits may be limited[13].

A number of biomedical interventions have been used for the treatment of autism and there is evidence that some medications can be effective for reducing problem behaviours such as severe aggression or hyperactivity and also for improving general functioning[3]. However, there are often undesirable side-effects associated with these medications. For example, the anti-psychotic drug risperidone is effective for controlling tantrums and self-injurious behaviours but its side-effects include weight gain, drowsiness and drooling[14]. There is some evidence that selective serotonin re-uptake inhibitors can improve mood and social interaction in people with autism, although this is inconclusive and they can result in side-effects such as restlessness, insomnia and nausea[15]. The stimulant methylphenidate can be used to treat hyperactivity[3]. It is worth noting that the purpose of psychopharmacological treatments for autism is to treat psychiatric symptoms associated with autism such as hyperactivity, aggression and self-injurious behaviour rather than the core features of autism[1].

# Summary points

- A number of interventions for autism have been developed.

- Applied behaviour analysis (ABA) is used to reinforce desirable behaviours and discourage undesirable ones.

- The TEACCH educational system was developed to take into account differences in how children with autism perceive the world.

- Augmentative and Alternative Communication (AAC) is designed to enable people with severe language difficulties to communicate via other means.

- Biomedical interventions can be used to improve general functioning of people with autism.

# Focus on: Experimental designs for testing interventions

In order to be able to assess the scientific evidence relating to an intervention, it is important to understand how the studies that the evidence comes from are designed. Experiments to test the effectiveness of interventions often have a 'group design'. This is where the participants in the study are randomly assigned to one of two groups. One group of individuals is provided with the intervention and the response to the intervention in this group is compared to the other (control) group that has either not received the intervention or has received a different intervention. The responses of the two groups are compared using statistics to determine whether the interventions have had a significant effect.

Group design studies have been used to provide evidence for or against interventions for autism. However, group designs can be problematic in autism research. They require having two randomly selected, but similar, groups for comparison, but due to the wide variability of autism symptoms, these two groups are likely to have large starting differences which can make it difficult to interpret the results of the experiment. Additionally, for children with autism, early and intensive intervention is recommended and the necessity of having an untreated control group for comparison in the experiment would mean that some children may be deprived of valuable interventions.

Because of these issues, in autism intervention research the most common type of experimental design involves using single individuals. Single-subject research designs (SSRD) involve making a comparison of one intervention with either another intervention, or no intervention at all, using the same individual. An SSRD study will typically take place over a number of sessions, with the initial sessions establishing a starting, or baseline, behaviour and later sessions involving the application of an intervention designed to modify the behaviour. A consistent improvement in behaviour during the phase when the intervention is applied provides evidence that the treatment is effective. The behaviours to be investigated are predetermined and relatively easy to quantify, such as picture-matching or play skills. SSRD are well established in the field of behavioural analysis and are useful for studies that aim to find differences among individuals in response to the effects of an intervention.

# References

1  Rogers, S J and Vismara, L A (2008) "Evidence-based comprehensive treatments for early autism." *Journal of Clinical Child & Adolescent Psychology*, 37(1), pp. 8–38.

2  Matson, J L, Konst, MJ (2013) "What is the evidence for long term effects of early autism interventions?" *Research in Autism Spectrum Disorders*, 7(3), pp. 475-479.

3  Francis, K (2005) "Autism interventions: a critical update." *Developmental Medicine and Child Neurology*, 47(7), pp. 493–499.

4  McConnell, S R (2002) "Interventions to facilitate social interaction for young children with autism: review of available research and recommendations for educational intervention and future research." *Journal of Autism and Developmental Disorders*, 32(5), pp. 351–372.

5  Odom, S L (2003) "Evidence-based practices for young children with autism." *Focus on Autism and Other Developmental Disabilities*, 18(3), pp. 166–175.

6  Ospina, M B, Krebs Seida, J, Clark, B, Karkhaneh, M, et al. (2008) "Behavioural and developmenal interventions for autism spectrum disorder: a clinical systematic review." *PLoS One*, 3(11), p. e3755.

7  Remington, B, Hastings, R P, Kovshoff, H, degli Espinosa, F, Jahr, E, Brown, T, Alsford, P, Lemaic, M, Ward, N (2007) "Early intensive behavioral intervention: Outcomes for children with autism and their parents after two years." *American Journal on Mental Retardation*, 112(6), pp. 418-438.

8  Magiati, I, Charman, T, Howlin, P (2007) "A two-year prospective follow-up study of community-based early intensive behavioural intervention and specialist nursery provision for children with autism spectrum disorders." *Journal of Child Psychology and Psychiatry*, 48(8), pp. 803-812.

9  Smith, T (1999) "Outcome of early intervention for children with autism." *Clinical Psychology: Science and Practice*, 6(1), pp. 33–49.

10  Ozonoff, S and Cathcart, K (1998) "Effectiveness of a home program intervention for young children with autism." *Journal of Autism and Developmental Disorders*, 28(1), pp. 25-32.

11  Hume, K and Odom, S (2007) "Effects of an individual work system on the independent functioning of students with autism." *Journal of Autism and Developmental Disorders*, 37(6), pp. 1166-1180.

12  Millar, D C, Light, J C and Schlosser, R W (2006) "The impact of augmentative and alternative communication intervention on the speech production of individuals with developmental disabilities: a research review." *Journal of Speech, Language, and Hearing Research*, 49(2), pp. 248-264.

13  Schlosser, R W (2008) "Effects of augmentative and alternative communication intervention on speech production in children with autism: a systematic review." *American Journal of Speech-Language Pathology*, 17(3), pp. 212-230.

14  McCracken, J T, McGough, J, Shah, B, Cronin, P, et al. (2002) "Risperidone in children with autism and serious behavioural problems." *New England Journal of Medicine*, 347(5), pp. 314-321.

15  Tsai, L Y (1999) "Psychopharmacology in autism." *Psychosomatic Medicine*, 61(5), pp. 651-665.

# Chapter 8:
# How 'good science' can be misinterpreted

As the awareness of autism increases, the desire for answers to its causes and how it can be treated has also increased. Many of the proposed causes and treatments of autism are popular but do not have supporting scientific evidence. Furthermore, autism is commonly misrepresented in the media. For example, one common popular belief is that people with autism typically have savant skills (exceptional skills when compared both to the general population and the person's other skills), a notion falsely promoted in the movies. It is also common for the mainstream press to exaggerate the findings of autism research and make sensationalist claims, particularly in relation to the usefulness of diagnostic markers and possible cures for autism.

As we will see in Chapter 9, the danger of irresponsible and sensationalist reporting is that it leads to further and sometimes potentially dangerous misconceptions about autism.

So far in this book we have reviewed some of the evidence-based research and have given an account of the current state of scientific thinking in relation to the causes and treatments of autism. It is now time to consider the 'bad science' aspect of autism. 'Bad science' in this context does not refer to genuine scientific studies that happen to have methodological shortcomings or conclusions that are not strongly supported – despite their weaknesses, such studies can sometimes provide some contribution to our understanding of a condition. It instead refers to ways of thinking about autism that are unsupported by the evidence but which retain popularity in spite of this. There are a considerable number of proposed causes and treatments of autism that are popular in the public sphere, but which either have little empirical data to support them or have been soundly shown to be false through scientific investigation. There may be a number of reasons for the persistence of such ideas in the face of scientific evidence, but the popular media is likely to play an important role as it is through the media that the general public acquire much of their information relating to autism.

The public awareness of autism and its coverage in the media have dramatically increased over time. Alongside this increased coverage are serious misunderstandings of the condition. Autism has been a popular subject in Hollywood movies, though they have a tendency to present autism as a psychological construction rather than as the neurological condition science has shown it to be[1]. There is also a fascination within movies with savant syndrome, exemplified by Dustin Hoffman's character in 'Rain Man', who has an array of savant skills, including the ability to memorise telephone books and decks of cards[2]. An impression that the general public may get from such media representation is that people with autism typically have some sort of 'special skills'. In reality, depending on how these are defined, only between 0.5% and 10% of people with autism have savant skills, and the majority of these are likely to be much less dramatic than those displayed in the movies[3,4].

There is also often a disconnect between the findings of autism science research and how these findings are reported in the media. One problematic aspect of the interface between science and the media is that scientists tend to be very careful about drawing strong conclusions from their research and tend to qualify their statements. This is because of the self-critical nature of science - it is an acknowledgement that theories are always open to modification in the light of new evidence, and strong statements about the workings of nature may be potentially contradicted by future research. On the other hand newspapers need to sell copies and the media can often generate more public interest by making dramatic assertions and creating controversy about scientific results.

Additionally, there is a disconnect between what the public learn about autism research through the media and the actual scientific research that is being performed[5]. The main areas of autism science research are brain development, genetics and treatments. However, the media typically focus on the environmental causes of autism, in particular the discredited vaccine-autism connection, as these issues propose a simple cause and effect: this resonates with the public more easily than the complex and nuanced reality. A disparity in reporting such as this may lead to public misunderstandings and poor decision-making in relation to the status of autism research.

One of the ways in which the media have exaggerated the results of autism research is in relation to the search for biomarkers of autism. One recent study that investigated brain structure in people with autism was widely reported in the popular press as having identified an accurate biomarker. Ecker *et al.* (2010) performed MRI scans on 20 adults with high-functioning autism or Asperger syndrome and compared various 'multidimensional' components of their brain structures with a control group of 20 adults without autism[6]. One of the

measurements, the thickness of the left hemisphere cortex, correctly classified up to 90% of all cases. This meant that 18 out of 20 people with autism were correctly classified as having autism and only 2 people without autism were incorrectly classified. This 90% accuracy rate was widely reported in the press as being an effective way to detect autism at an early age (eg. BBC News Aug 10 2010; Daily Mail, Aug 11 2010).

Although this study certainly contributed to autism research, its value as a diagnostic tool was over-estimated. Remember that the great majority of people in the general population (about 99%) do not have autism. This means that if you were to take 100 random people from the population, on average only 1 person would have autism. If the diagnostic test were applied to all 100 people, there would indeed be a high (90%) chance of correctly identifying the 1 person who had autism. However, a number of people who do not have autism (about 10) would also be **incorrectly** identified as having autism. In other words, after all 100 people had been tested, the end result would be about 11 people identified as having autism, but only 1 actually having autism. Separating out the 1 person with autism from the 10 without would be a major challenge! The more people tested, the more incorrect identifications would be made, meaning that this test would certainly not be suitable for screening the general population for autism.

Although it was not the 'breakthrough' that was reported in the press, the Ecker et al. (2010) study was good research in that it increased our understanding of how the brains of people with autism differ in structure and it is possible that the methods used in the study could be useful for complementing standard diagnostic techniques. However, although it was widely reported in the media, the statistical issues with the study as well as its small size and preliminary nature were not discussed. This may have misled the public into thinking that autism can now be detected using a 15 minute brain scan, as claimed by the Daily Express (Aug 11 2010).

Another study that generated a lot of media excitement involved using the automated analysis of vocalisations to screen for autism. Oller et al. (2010) recorded and analysed the vocal patterns of 77 children with autism compared to 106 typically-developing children and found that there were a number of pitch and rhythm differences associated with autism[7]. A number of media reports emphasised the potential of this method as a screening tool for autism (Telegraph Jul 19 2010; BBC, Jul 20 2010; Daily Mail, Jul 21 2010). However, again, the problem with the study was that it was designed to contain a high proportion of children with autism. If the number of children with autism had

reflected the rate of 1% in the general population then there would be a higher number of people incorrectly diagnosed with autism than the number of people correctly diagnosed using this screening tool. Additionally, the study found that there was a strong degree of overlap between autism and other language-impaired groups, suggesting that vocal abnormalities are not unique signatures of autism. The technique used in the study may not be very useful on its own for diagnosing autism in children but could perhaps supplement the psychological tests currently used for diagnoses. Other than clinical applications, the Oller et al. (2010) research was useful for understanding the development of speech in children.

Another study by Yap et al. (2010) attempted to use the chemical profile of urine as a biomarker for autism. It found that the urine of children with autism had some chemical differences compared to children without autism[8]. However, the sample size used in the study was small and there was a lot of variation among all of the children regardless of whether they had autism. As a diagnostic tool, it is too early to say whether urine tests would be useful for the screening of autism. Nevertheless, the media presented this research as being a breakthrough and as a simple test with a 'yes or no' answer (Daily Mail, Jun 4 2010; The Daily Telegraph, Jun 4 2010).

## Summary points

- Many proposed causes and treatments of autism are popular but do not have supporting evidence.
- Autism is commonly misrepresented in the media, such as by presenting people with autism as commonly having savant skills.
- The press often exaggerates the findings of autism research, particularly in relation to the usefulness of diagnostic markers.

### References

1 Murray, S (2006) "Autism and the contemporary sentimental: fiction and the narrative fascination of the present." *Literature and Medicine*, 25(1), pp. 24–45.

2 Draaisma, D (2009) "Stereotypes of autism." *Philosophical Transactions of the Roal Society B: Biological Sciences*, 364(1522), pp. 1475–1480.

3 Treffert, D A (2009) "The savant syndrome: an extraordinary condition. A synopsis: past, present, future." *Philosophical Transactions of the Roal Society B: Biological Sciences*, 364(1522), pp. 1351–1357.

4 NAS (2007) Think differently - act positively

5 Singh, J, Hallmayer, J and Illes, J (2007) "Interacting and paradoxical forces in neuroscience and society." *Nature Reviews Neuroscience*, 8(2), pp. 153–160.

6 Ecker, C, Marquand, A, Mourao-Miranda, J, Johnston, P, et al. (2010) "Describing the brain in autism in five dimensions - magnetic resonance imaging-assisted diagnosis of autism spectrum disorder using a multiparameter classification approach." *The Journal of Neuroscience*, 30(32), pp. 10612–10623.

7 Oller, D K, Niyogi, P, Gray, S, Richards, J A, et al. (2010) "Automated vocal analysis of naturalistic recordings from children with autism, language delay, and typical development." *Proceedings of the National Academy of Sciences*, 107(30), pp. 13354–13359.

8  Yap, I K S, Angley, M, Veselkov, K A, Holmes, E, et al. (2010) "Urinary metabolic phenotyping differentiates children with autism from their unaffected siblings and age-matched controls." *Journal of Proteome Research*, 9(6), pp. 2996–3004.

# Chapter 9:
# Bad science in relation to the causes of autism

One of the best examples of how bad science can have a major negative impact in the public sphere is that of the MMR scandal. In 1998, a publication later determined to be fraudulent claimed to have found an association between immunisation with the MMR vaccine and the onset of autism in a small group of children. Biased reporting by the media, along with ineffective communication by scientists and the government, led to a reduction in the uptake of MMR, which in turn led to a surge in the number of cases of measles. Since then, many large scale studies performed across the world have found that there is no connection between the MMR vaccine and autism, although this has not prevented this discredited idea from continuing to be promoted on the internet and occasionally in the popular press.

Apart from MMR, vaccines have been linked to autism in other ways. In the US in particular, there has been speculation that the preservative thimoseral, used as a preservative in some vaccines, might cause autism. However, once again numerous carefully performed research studies have shown that this proposed connection is unsubstantiated.

This chapter aims to highlight how bad science can have a negative impact on public health and perceptions of autism and how it can result in a misdirection of resources for autism research.

O ther than misrepresenting autism science research the media has played a far more damaging role in promoting health scares surrounding autism. Probably the greatest tragedy resulting from the 'bad science' of autism research and the failure of effective science communication to the public is the autism-vaccine controversy. In this case the media has been responsible to a large degree for promoting the myth that vaccines are responsible for causing autism. This has led to a major reduction in vaccination uptake and a corresponding increase in the occurrence of serious diseases in the UK and US.

In 1998 a controversial study was published that proposed a link between autism and the MMR vaccine[1]. The researchers involved investigated 12 children who exhibited a number of symptoms of gastrointestinal disorders and developmental setbacks. The paper described these symptoms as developing soon after the children received the MMR vaccination. The researchers claimed to have identified a distinctive inflammatory bowel condition, later dubbed "autistic enterocolitis", in the children involved in the study. The hypothesis proposed by the paper was

**Vaccines and MMR:**
Vaccines are one of the greatest inventions in medical history. The consensus of the medical community and the government is that vaccines are safe. However, historically, there has been a degree of mistrust of vaccines by the British public as well as of the claims of the government and health officials[6]. The MMR (measles, mumps and rubella) vaccine was introduced into the UK in 1988 and now is in widespread use around the world[11]. It is administered in two doses, one at 12-15 months and one at 3-5 years to maximise its effectiveness.

that, following injection, MMR passed to the gut and caused gastric problems and then travelled to the brain triggering autism. Following the publication of the paper the lead author, Andrew Wakefield, held a press conference at which he announced that the MMR vaccine was potentially harmful and that the use of single vaccinations would be more appropriate.

Shortly after it was published the scientific limitations of Wakefield's paper became apparent[2]. In terms of methodology, the study used a very small sample size (12 children), from which it would be difficult to generalise. It did not use a control group and relied to a large extent on the subjective beliefs and recollections of the parents[3]. Further issues with the paper came to light when a journalist, Brian Deer, published a number of investigations in the Sunday Times describing elements of fraud, unethical treatment of children and conflicts of interest in the research (Sunday Times, Feb 22, 2004). Deer discovered that Wakefield had filed a patent application for a rival vaccine that was intended to replace MMR. Additionally, two years before Wakefield's 1998 paper was published, he was paid about $700,000 by a law firm that was building a case to sue vaccine makers. Deer also found evidence of data falsification in the 1998 paper, in that all of the 12 cases reported were misrepresented in terms of diagnoses and medical histories. In 6 of the cases, the developmental problems reported were actually present before the MMR vaccine was first administered. There was also a question-mark over whether some of the children really had gastrointestinal problems as there was initial disagreement over the pathology reports from the hospital where the study was performed that went unreported. The laboratory analysis of the gut tissue samples used in the study had not been performed correctly and the results of this analysis were questionable and should not have been reported. Taken together, there were major problems with the Wakefield (1998) paper and it is unsurprising that it was eventually retracted[4]. The retraction followed a forensic analysis of the paper by the General Medical Council (the regulatory body of medical practitioners in the UK) who ruled that Wakefield had deliberately misled The Lancet about the nature of the research[5]. Retractions of scientific and medical papers are rare and only occur when major problems or evidence of fraud are discovered but in this case it was clear that there were major scientific and ethical flaws with Wakefield's research.

The Wakefield (1998) paper and subsequent press conference went relatively unnoticed by the media at the time. Two more papers co-authored by Wakefield in 2000 and 2002 claimed to have identified measles virus in the tissue of people with bowel problems and autism[7,8]. The results of these studies were later called into question and were demonstrated to have probably been due to errors in carrying out the experimentation[9]. However, the following year the media began to devote considerable attention to the autism–vaccine 'controversy'. Although the original Wakefield paper was thoroughly discredited and retracted in 2010 it was widely publicised by the press[10]. Anti-vaccination campaigners presented distraught parents who gave anecdotes about how their children regressed into autism after having received the MMR vaccine. These accounts were contrasted with rather dry, terse statements from doctors and government health officials who declared the vaccine to be safe. Statements from authority figures on both sides were presented in the press without any critical evaluation of the evidence supporting either side. Many reports in the media presented both sides of the controversy equally, which gave credibility to the vaccine-autism theory and created a perception among the public that there was equal evidence to support both sides[11]. This problem was exacerbated in December 2001 when the then Prime Minister Tony Blair refused to say whether his infant son had been given the MMR vaccine, despite the government's assurances that it was safe.

The MMR controversy peaked in 2002 when the subject of MMR and autism became the most popular science issue to be covered in the press[10]. Newspapers began to take editorial stances on the MMR-autism debate and media celebrities were given platforms to voice their opinions on vaccine safety. Thus, the question of whether MMR was responsible for autism, which should be approached scientifically, became highly politicised and emotive and was addressed in the public domain more by feelings than by evidence.

In response to the growing concern about MMR and the reduced uptake in vaccination that resulted from this, a number of large-scale epidemiological studies were carried out to try to determine whether the association of MMR and autism was genuine. The MMR vaccine is administered around the time that children often begin to show the characteristic symptoms of autism. Although it may seem intuitively plausible that such a correlation indicates a causative role for MMR in producing autism it could also be due to coincidence and the role of scientific investigation is to determine objectively whether there is a genuine cause and effect taking place. Smeeth et al. (2004) performed a 'case-control' study in which a large group of children with autism were compared to another large group without autism in the UK to determine whether MMR vaccination was more common in either group[12]. There was no difference in the rate of MMR vaccination among the children with autism compared to those without.

A number of 'time-trend' studies were performed where researchers investigated whether the rate of autism changed over time relative to the introduction of MMR. Taylor et al. (1999) evaluated several hundred children with autism who were born between 1979 and 1992 in the UK and found that there was no change in the rate of autism diagnoses following the introduction of MMR in 1987 and also that there were no differences in the rates of autism among vaccinated and unvaccinated children[13]. Kaye et al. (2001) found that in the years following the introduction of MMR in the UK (1988-1999), although the prevalence increased over time, there was no corresponding increase in the rate of MMR vaccination which remained stable[14].

Other than in the UK, numerous epidemiological studies have been carried out to investigate a potential link between autism and MMR. In Denmark, a large 'cohort' study was performed by Madsen *et al.* (2002) which compared a group of children that had received the MMR vaccination to a group that had not received it[15]. This study involved hundreds of thousands of children and no difference was found in the rates of autism between vaccinated and unvaccinated children. Other studies from Finland[16], Sweden[17], United States[18] and Japan[19] have consistently failed to find any association between MMR and autism.

This accumulated epidemiological research, as well as the retraction of the original Wakefield (1998) paper should have conclusively settled the MMR-autism issue. However, despite the overwhelming evidence against a role of MMR in causing autism, many parents continue to be sceptical about the safety of vaccines[20]. This is perhaps partly due to the new values of the media. Saying (wrongly) that MMR is linked to autism is news; saying (correctly) that MMR is not linked to autism is less of a news story - and there is also not much incentive for the media to admit if they get it wrong[21].

A large amount of media coverage was given to a small number of researchers such as Andrew Wakefield and Arthur Krigsman who made unsubstantiated claims that they had discovered evidence for an autism-MMR connection[22]. These claims were reported in the press but not in peer-reviewed journals, where they could be analysed by other researchers and so could not be independently evaluated. In addition, there is a very active and vocal anti-vaccination movement to whom the retraction of the Wakefield (1998) paper reinforces the idea that there is a conspiracy among the medical establishment to suppress dissenting voices. To these people Wakefield is something of a martyr figure, being persecuted by the 'system' for daring to speak out. Wakefield himself refused to admit any wrongdoing and although he has been struck from the medical register in the UK, continues to promote his views in the US[23].

There are vocal anti-vaccination groups active in the UK and US that continue to promote the autism-vaccine connection. There are several hundred anti-vaccination websites on the internet. In the US, major anti-vaccination groups include 'Generation Rescue' and 'Age of Autism'. Although it is unsupported in terms of scientific evidence, the anti-vaccination movement has been highly successful in terms of public relations. For example, Jenny McCarthy is a US celebrity, actress and former Playboy model who is active in the US anti-vaccination movement and has received a significant amount of attention in the mainstream press for claiming that vaccines were responsible for causing autism in her son. She also claims to have cured her son's autism using a number of non-scientific, alternative treatments. McCarthy has appeared on numerous widely viewed US chat shows and news programs, such as 'Oprah', 'Larry King', 'Good Morning America', and others.

Driven by inaccurate media reporting and ineffective responses from the government and the medical establishment, the autism-MMR controversy has caused considerable damage to public health[24]. Despite assurances from the government about the safety of vaccines, vaccination rates in the UK hit a record low of about 80% in 2003 – 2004 (Health Protection Agency, www.hpa.org.uk). Although there has been an increase in vaccination uptake since then, as of 2011, vaccination rates are still below the level recommended by the World Health Organisation for herd immunity.

As a result of the autism-MMR panic, there are hundreds of thousands of unvaccinated children at risk of preventable infectious disease in the UK. The diseases that MMR immunises against are not trivial ones. Measles is a highly contagious viral disease that can be transmitted without direct contact. Its main symptoms are a high fever and a rash, but in about 1 in 15 children who contract the disease more serious complications develop which can include seizures, blindness and brain damage. Measles can also result in death and, prior to the introduction of mass vaccination, was responsible for about 100 deaths per year in the UK[25].

As a result of reduced vaccination rates the numbers of measles cases in the UK have dramatically increased and at present are at the highest levels since current surveillance methods were introduced in 1995. There have been a number of large outbreaks of measles in some areas[26], particularly in London, and in 2006 the first fatality from measles in over a decade occurred in the UK (Sunday Times, Apr 2, 2006). In 2012, the

## Herd immunity:

The concept that if a sufficiently large proportion (about 85 – 90%) of the population is immunised against a disease the levels of transmission of the disease will be greatly reduced, it will be unable to spread and will eventually become extinct. There will always be a small percentage of people who cannot receive vaccinations for a variety of reasons, such as having poor health or particularly weak immune systems. These people are often especially at risk of infectious disease. Through herd immunity, they would be protected due to the immunity of the rest of the population.

Health Protection Agency reported the highest number of cases of measles in 18 years, with 2016 cases reported (http://www.bbc.co.uk/news/health-21381274). The number of cases of mumps, a common cause of viral meningitis, and rubella, which presents a danger to the unborn children of infected mothers[27], has also risen dramatically from less than a hundred before 1999 to thousands today. However, despite reduced vaccination rates the observed prevalence of autism has continued to rise, probably driven by increased awareness and changes to diagnostic criteria as described earlier.

In the UK, concern over vaccinations has focussed on MMR, whereas in the US, the main target of the anti-vaccination movement has been the use of mercury-based preservatives in vaccinations. This idea stems from a theoretical proposal, rather than a scientific article, published in 2001 speculating that excess levels of thimerosal exposure from vaccines may cause autism[28]. Thimerosal is a preservative that has been used in vaccines since the 1930s and is composed of about 50% mercury[29]. In the US in the late 1990s, there was some concern by the government that the levels of mercury contained in vaccines could potentially be harmful and the preservative thimerosal was eventually removed from vaccines[30]. Although mercury is a known neurotoxin, whether it causes actual harm is dependent

on the dosage. The ban on thimerosal was based not on any supporting evidence that the dosage administered was harmful but was based on the 'precautionary principle' - removing it 'just in case' it may have harmful effects. This decision may nevertheless have contributed to the subsequent antagonism to the use of mercury in vaccines by the anti-vaccination movement[31]. For the public's perception, it seemed to indicate that there may have been some real danger from thimerosal, otherwise the government would have no reason to remove it[31].

As with the MMR vaccine, a number of studies were performed to evaluate whether there was a connection between thimerosal exposure and autism and the results of these consistently showed that there was no association. For example, Price *et al.* (2010) conducted a case-control study to compare two groups of children, one that had autism and the other without, and found that there was no difference in the levels of exposure to thimerosal between either group[29]. Additionally a number of 'before and after' studies were performed on the safety of thimerosal. Since thimerosal was effectively eliminated from vaccines in the US by 2002 it was predicted that if it was involved in causing autism there should have been a drop in autism prevalence after this time. Schechter & Grether (2008) conducted a time-trend study on the prevalence of autism in children from 1995 to 2007 and found that the prevalence of autism continued to rise over this timeframe and that there was no drop in prevalence after the time when thimerosal was removed from vaccines[32]. Finally, there have been a number of large-scale studies in countries around the world that have shown no association between thimerosal-containing vaccines and autism[33-35].

Despite the lack of evidence for an involvement of vaccines in causing autism, claims by parents that vaccinations led to their children developing autism have made their way to the courts. In 2007, a trial began in the US Court of Federal Claims that involved almost 5,000 lawsuits filed by families claiming that MMR and thimerosal in vaccines were responsible for their children's autism[36]. As a result of the huge number of claims, they were linked together into a 'class action suit' which became known as the Omnibus Autism Proceeding. Three 'test cases' were designated for each of two theories of 'general causation'- one that MMR and thimerosal-containing vaccines cause autism in combination and the other that thimerosal-containing vaccines alone cause autism. After the attorneys and a number of experts representing the families made their arguments the court rulings on all six cases conclusively found no evidence

between autism and vaccines meaning that no compensation was to be paid to the families. Thousands of cases remain open but these must now be resolved on an individual basis where a theory of causation must be submitted and supported.

Ideally, the verdicts of the Omnibus Autism Proceeding should persuade parents that there is no connection between vaccines and autism. Ultimately however, the question of whether vaccines cause autism is a scientific, rather than a legal, one. Numerous studies have addressed the issue and have found no connection. The discredited connection between vaccines and MMR has diverted huge amounts of time, energy and money away from useful studies into the genuine causes of autism[37].

## Summary points

- A major health scare in the UK has been the false association of the MMR vaccine with autism.
- This began with a fraudulent publication in 1998 that claimed to have found an association between immunisation with the MMR vaccine and the onset of autism in a small group of children.
- Biased reporting by the media, along with ineffective communication by scientists and the government, led to a reduction in the uptake of MMR.
- This in turn led to a surge in the number of cases of measles.
- Large scale studies have found that there is no connection between MMR and autism.
- In the US, concern about vaccines and autism has focussed on thimerosal but again science has shown that there is no connection.

**References**

1 Wakefield, A, Murch, S, Anthony, A, Linnell, J, et al. (1998) "Ileal-lymphoid-nodular hyperplasia, non-specific colitis, and pervasive developmental disorder in children." *The Lancet*, 351(9103), pp. 637–641.

2 Chen, R T and DeStefano, F (1998) "Vaccine adverse events: causal or coincidental?" *The Lancet*, 351(9103), pp. 611–612.

3 Payne, C and Mason, B (1998) "Autism, inflammatory bowel disease, and MMR vaccine." *The Lancet*, 351(9106), p. 907.

4 Anon (2010) "Retraction—Ileal-lymphoid-nodular hyperplasia, non-specific colitis, and pervasive developmental disorder in children." *The Lancet*, 375(9713), p. 445.

5 GMC (2010) "Dr Andrew Jeremy Wakefield: determination on Serious Professional Misconduct (SPM) and saction."

6 Singh, J, Hallmayer, J and Illes, J (2007) "Interacting and paradoxical forces in neuroscience and society." *Nature Reviews Neuroscience*, 8(2), pp.153-160.

7  Kawashima, H, Mori, T, Kashiwagi, Y, Takekuma, K, et al. (2000) "Detection and sequencing of measles virus from peripheral mononuclear cells from patients with inflammatory bowel disease and autism." *Digestive Diseases and Sciences*, 45(4), pp. 723–729.

8  Uhlmann, V, Martin, C M, Sheils, O, Pilkinton, L, Silva, I, Killalea, A, Murch, S B, Walker-Smith, J, Thomson, M, Wakefield, A J, O'Leary, J J (2002) "Potential viral pathogenic mechanism for new variant inflammatory bowel disease." *Molecular Pathology*, 55(2), pp. 84-90.

9  D'Souza, Y, Fombonne, E and Ward, B J (2006) "No evidence of persisting measles virus in peripeheral blood mononuclear cells from children with autism spectrum disorder." *Pediatrics*, 118(4), pp. 1664–1675.

10  Smith, M J, Ellenberg, S S, Bell, L M and Rubin, D M (2008) "Media coverage of the measles-mumps-rubella vaccine and autism controversy and its relationship to MMR immunization rates in the United States." *Pediatrics*, 121(4), pp. e836–e843.

11  Lewis, J and Speers, T (2003) "Misleading media reporting? The MMR story." *Nature Reviews Immunology*, 3(11), pp. 913–918.

12  Smeeth, L, Cook, C, Fombonne, E, Heavey, L, et al. (2004) "MMR vaccination and pervasive developmental disorders: a case-control study." *The Lancet*, 364(9438), pp. 963–969.

13  Taylor, B, Miller, E, Farrington, C P, Petropoulos, M C, et al. (1999) "Autism and measles, mumps, and rubella vaccine: no epidemiological evidence for a causal association." *The Lancet*, 363(9169), pp. 2026–2029.

14  Kaye, J A, Del Mar Melero-Montes, M and Jick, H (2001) "Mumps, measles, and rubella vaccine and the incidence of autism recorded by general practitioners: a time trend analysis." *British Medical Journal*, 322(7284), pp. 460–463.

15  Madsen, K M, Hviid, A, Vestergaard, M, Schendel, D, et al. (2002) "A population-based study of measles, mumps, and rubella vaccination and autism." *The New England Journal of Medicine*, 347(19), pp. 1477–1482.

16  Makela, A, Nuorti, J P and Peltola, H (2002) "Neurologic disorders after measles-mumps-rubella vaccination." *Pediatrics*, 110(5), pp. 957–963.

17  Gillberg, C and Heijbel, H (1998) "MMR and autism." *Autism*, 2(4), pp. 423–424.

18  Dales, L, Hammer, S J and Smith, N J (2001) "Time trends in autism and in MMR immunization coverage in California." *Journal of the American Medical Association*, 285(9), pp. 1183–1185.

19  Honda, H, Shimizu, Y and Rutter, M (2005) "No effect of MMR withdrawal on the incidence of autism: a total population study." *Journal of Child Psychology and Psychiatry*, 46(6), pp. 572–579.

20  Shevell, M and Fombonne, E (2006) "Autism and MMR vaccination or thimerosal exposure: an urban legend?" *Canadian Journal of Neurological Science*, 33(4), pp. 339–340.

21  Offit, P A and Coffin, S E (2003) "Communicating science to the public: MMR vaccine and autism." *Vaccine*, 22(1), pp. 1–6.

22  Goldacre, B (2008) *Bad Science*, London, Harper Collins.

23  BMJ (2011) "In the wake of Wakefield." *British Medical Journal*, 342, p. d806.

24  Bedford, H E and Elliman, D A C (2010) "MMR vaccine and autism." *British Medical Journal*, 340, p. c655.

25  Gay, N J, Hesketh, L M, Morgan-Capner, P and Miller, E (1995) "Interpretation of serological surveillance data for measles using mathematical models: implications for vaccine strategy." *Epidemology and Infection*, 115(1), pp. 139–156.

26  Jansen, V A A, Stollenwek, N, J, Jensen H, Ramsay, M E, et al. (2003) "Measles outbreaks in a population with declining vaccine uptake." *Science*, 301(5634), p. 804.

27  Miller, E (2002) "MMR vaccine: review of benefits and risks." *The Journal of Infection*, 44(1), pp. 1–6.

28  Bernard, S, Enayati, A, Redwood, L, Roger, H and Binstock, T (2001) "Autism: a novel form of mercury poisoning." *Medical Hypotheses*, 56(4), pp. 462–471.

29  Price, C S, Thompson, W W, Goodson, B, Weintraub, E S, et al. (2010) "Prenatal and infant exposure to thimerosal from vaccines and immunoglobulins and risk of autism." *Pediatrics*, 126(4), pp. 656–664.

30  CDC (1999) "Thimerosal in vaccines: a joint statement of the Americal Academy of Pediatrics and the Public Health Service." *MMWR Morbidity and Mortality Weekly Report*, 48(6), pp. 563–565.

31  Gerber, J S and Offit, P A (2009) "Vaccines and autism: a tale of shifting hypotheses." *Clinical Infectious Diseases*, 48(4), pp. 456–461.

32  Schechter, R and Grether, J K (2008) "Continuing increases in autism reported to California's developmental services system." *Archives of General Psychiatry*, 65(1), pp. 19–24.

33  Hviid, A, Stellfeld, M, Wohlfahrt, J and Melbye, M (2003) "Association between thimerosal-containing vaccine and autism." *JAMA : the journal of the American Medical Association*, 290(13), pp. 1763–6.

34  Andrews, N, Miller, E, Grant, A, Stowe, J, et al. (2004) "Thimerosal exposure in infants and developmental disorders: a retrospective cohort study in the United kingdom does not support a causal association." *Pediatrics*, 114(3), pp. 584–91.

35  Verstraeten, T, L, Davis R, DeStefano, F, Lieu, T A, et al. (2003) "Safety of thimerosal-containing vaccines: a two-phased study of computerized health maintenance organization databases." *Pediatrics*, 112(5), pp. 1039–1048.

36  Cook, K M and Evans, G (2011) "The National Vaccine Injury Compensation Program." *Pediatrics*, 127(Suppl 1), pp. S74–S77.

37  Oakley Jr., G P and Johnston Jr., R B (2004) "Balancing benefits and harms in public health prevention programmes mandated by governments." *British Medical Journal*, 329(7456), pp. 41–44.

# Chapter 10:
# The search for treatments for autism

Alongside conventional medicine, a wide range of complementary and alternative medicines (CAM) have become popular. However, there tends to be very little evidence to support their use. Some CAM therapies are based on scientifically implausible mechanisms of action, while others, such as hyperbaric oxygen therapy and chelation therapy, have potentially dangerous side-effects. Some treatments, such as the use of secretin, initially showed promise. However, after extensive studies were undertaken it was shown that secretin did not improve the symptoms of autism. In some cases, such as the use of the gluten-free casein-free diet, there is a lot of anecdotal report of improvements in behaviour as a result of this diet being used. Nevertheless, there is still insufficient scientific evidence to back up such claims. Finally, in some cases, the treatments are relatively harmless, such as interacting with dolphins or horses and although there is anecdotal evidence that some people with autism respond well to these interventions, they may not be generally effective. Further research on CAM treatments is underway and there are some good online resources available to help parents find out whether treatments they are considering are backed up by scientific evidence and safe for their children.

This chapter considers some of the most popular CAM therapies currently in use and the approach parents should use in evaluating their safety and any claims of effectiveness that have been made.

In the absence of any scientifically-validated, straightforward 'cure' for autism a wide range of unconventional therapies have become popular. These include complementary medicines, which are typically used alongside conventional medicine, as well as alternative medicines, which are used in place of it. Complementary and alternative medicines (CAM) together have been defined by the National Center for Complementary and Alternative Medicine (NCCAM) as a 'group of diverse medical and health care systems, practices, and products that are not presently considered to be part of conventional medicine' (www.nccam.nih.gov/health/whatiscam). The use of CAM has risen steadily over the years and is now popular throughout the industrialised world[1]. In the US, a study showed that as many as three-quarters of families with a child with autism tried some form of CAM[2].

There are a number of potential reasons why CAM may appeal to the parents of children with autism. The age of the internet has greatly increased the exposure of families affected by autism to many proposed 'miracle' cures based on unsubstantiated claims and testimonials[3]. Conventional interventions have not been effective for treating the core symptoms of autism and this could lead to disillusionment for some parents who may turn to CAM for alternatives[3]. Certain CAM may be perceived as being less invasive and simpler to implement than conventional interventions[4] as well as potentially having fewer side-effects[2]. CAM may appeal more to parents as they are often portrayed as being more 'natural' remedies in comparison to the 'artificial' and 'manufactured' treatments used in conventional medicine[2]. CAM may be seen as being less authoritarian than conventional medicine and as offering patients more autonomy over decisions they can make regarding healthcare. It may also be easier to acquire access to CAM as they usually do not require prior approval or prescriptions[2]. The increasing use of CAM by the public may reflect a broader philosophical perspective that aims to incorporate more 'holistic' or 'spiritual' components to life[4].

There are a large number of CAM therapies for autism currently used. There is a great deal of variability among these but they can be grouped into several general categories. Some therapies are based around manipulation of various parts of the body. Other therapies aim to channel particular 'energy fields' that practitioners believe penetrate and surround the body. Some CAM therapies for autism involve supplementing the diet with various natural products such as vitamins or herbs. There are also CAM therapies that are based on the idea that the mind can strongly influence the body with regard to overcoming symptoms. The various CAM therapies for autism differ in terms of popularity and the popularity of a given treatment can quickly change over time[2].

Considering the multitude of interventions for autism that are available, the decision as to which one to use for their child must be daunting for parents. It is critical that a fully informed choice is made - parents, as well as medical practitioners, should be aware of the extent to which a particular intervention has been shown to be safe and effective in peer-reviewed scientific studies.

Many CAM therapies are based on unconventional theories and are unsupported by any clinical research[3]. They are often based on implausible principles of mechanism that contradict current scientific understanding and are supported primarily by anecdotal, rather than empirical, evidence[3]. Many of the CAM treatments for autism have not been adequately researched using scientific approaches[5]. An important role of science in autism research is to help people with autism themselves, their parents and care-providers to be able to evaluate the effectiveness of unproven treatments. Well designed scientific studies can be used to investigate whether anecdotal reports regarding the success of CAM treatments hold any weight. Additionally, scientific studies can be used to determine any possible negative effects that may be caused

by CAM therapies. Some CAM therapies may actually be harmful and result in health problems for receivers, such as by leading to dietary deficiencies, causing direct toxicity, or by interrupting or postponing genuinely effective therapies[3]. It is beyond the scope of this book to discuss all of the CAM therapies that are promoted for the treatment of autism but a few of the more popular ones will now be examined.

Some CAM treatments for autism involve making alterations to the diet but there is little scientific evidence in support of these. One of the most popular treatments for autism is the gluten-free, casein-free diet (GFCF)[6]. This is based on the theory that some of the symptoms of autism are the result of peptides that form as a result of the incomplete breakdown of the proteins gluten and casein. The theory postulates that these peptides enter the bloodstream from the intestine and are transported to the brain, where they affect the nervous system and lead to behaviours associated with autism. There are many anecdotal reports from parents of their children showing improvements in sociability and reduction in aggression when placed on GFCF diets, but these remain to be supported by large, randomised and controlled scientific studies[7]. It is also possible that such tightly restricted diets could be harmful, by leading to inadequate nutrition, and there is a certain level of cost and stress associated with maintaining GFCF diets[8]. More research is needed to determine the effectiveness of GFCF diets and a number of clinical trials are currently underway[6].

Another way in which diet is sometimes manipulated to attempt to treat autism is by supplementation with vitamins and/or minerals. Again, there is little scientific evidence to support these treatments, although they often receive anecdotal support from parents who have provided them to their children. A number of early studies had positive results but these tended to be methodologically weak, such as not being randomised or having control groups[9]. Only a few rigorous studies have been performed to assess the effects of vitamin B6 and magnesium supplementation together and these failed to show any benefit[9].

There have been a few cases where a CAM therapy has received some support from one or a few scientific studies. These results will often be reported in the press as being strong, or even conclusive, evidence that the treatment is effective. For example, hyperbaric oxygen therapy, which is commonly used to treat decompression sickness, involves placing a patient inside a pressurised chamber which is then used to deliver oxygen at a high pressure to increase the rate of oxygen absorption in the blood. Hyperbaric oxygen therapy is also used as a CAM therapy for children with

autism, although there is little theoretical basis for understanding how increased oxygen absorption could affect the symptoms of autism. A single group design study showed that this therapy resulted in positive changes to the behaviour of children with autism[10].

This study had the hallmarks of a well designed experiment and following its publication, newspapers widely reported the positive results. However, the strength of an idea in science depends on the body of the evidence that supports it and a single, relatively small study alone provides insufficient evidence to fully accept the effectiveness of hyperbaric oxygen therapy in the treatment of autism[10]. The results of a positive trial should be replicated (the same results should be obtained when the study is repeated) ideally by a different research team that should repeat the experiment using fresh groups of subjects to ensure that the results are consistent. The more times the results of study have been replicated, the more confident we can be that they are consistent and reliable. At best the study was a promising result which should be followed up by further research. Further research has in fact been carried out and so far has failed to replicate the positive results[11,12]. Hyperbaric oxygen therapy is expensive and can have side-effects such as causing damage to the inner ear. A single, small, unreplicated study that supports it should not be taken as strong evidence for its effectiveness. Some CAM treatments have started out as being considered promising in both conventional medicine and CAM domains but as research demonstrated their ineffectiveness their popularities have declined. For example, the chemical secretin was proposed as being a cure for autism[2]. The normal use of secretin is to test gastrointestinal functioning in adults. There was intense media interest into secretin with a focus on anecdotal reports of success. A large number of studies were subsequently performed to determine whether secretin was actually an effective treatment for the symptoms of autism. Secretin was administered to hundreds of children diagnosed with autism who were then assessed for effects[5]. Almost all of these studies failed to find any relationship between secretin and a reduction in the symptoms of autism[5]. Millions of dollars were spent on research into the effectiveness of secretin for autism treatment and the evidence strongly suggested that it was ineffective. Despite these results, there is still a demand by some parents for secretin.

Some therapies, while not having been scientifically demonstrated to work, are likely to be relatively harmless. For example, therapies involving the interaction of children with autism with animals such as dolphins and horses may be enjoyable for the child, even if they have not been scientifically shown

to be effective for treating the symptoms of autism. However, other CAM therapies for autism can have dangerous side-effects. Chelation therapy is a treatment that is used in cases where a patient suffers from heavy metal poisoning. Heavy metals cannot be broken down by the body and can in some cases build up to dangerous levels. Chelation therapy involves the oral or intravenous administration of a chemical called EDTA that binds to the heavy metal atoms and facilitates their removal from the body through urine. Apart from its mainstream use chelation therapy has become popular as an alternative treatment for a wide range of conditions such as diabetes, arthritis, multiple sclerosis and autism. The idea behind using chelation therapy as a treatment for autism is based on the discredited theory that a build-up of mercury contained within vaccines is responsible for causing autism[13]. However, there is no evidence that chelation therapy is effective for treating any condition other than heavy metal poisoning. In fact, it has been shown to cause health problems such as nausea, lowering of the blood pressure, kidney damage and impairments to the immune system. There are a number of serious side effects associated with chelation therapy and there has been at least one fatality of a child with autism resulting from it[14]. For these reasons, a proposed study by the National Institute of Mental Health in the US into the effectiveness of chelation therapy for the treatment of autism was cancelled as 'there was no clear evidence for direct benefit to the children who would participate in the chelation trial and that the study presents more than a minimal risk' (Wall Street Journal 18 Sep, 2008). Despite the increasing popularity of chelation therapy in the CAM community the fact that it is based on a disproven theory and has no supporting evidence and has potential health risks means that it should not be used as a treatment for autism[15].

One non-biological intervention for autism that is sometimes used is facilitated communication (FC). This is a treatment for non-verbal people in which a 'facilitator' guides their hand to a computer or other spelling device in order to enable them to communicate. FC was initially heralded as a breakthrough in enabling non-verbal people to be able to express their thoughts and feelings. However, although proponents of FC often cite anecdotal support, single-subject studies have shown that FC does not work and that, in most cases it is the facilitator, whether subconsciously or consciously, that is actually communicating[16]. To date there have been several dozen scientific studies as well as a number of court cases that have shown that FC is unreliable and ineffective and can also potentially cause harm in cases where "facilitated" communication has made unfounded criminal accusations against family members of the person being facilitated[17].

In evaluating treatments for autism there are a number of characteristics or 'warning signs' that pseudoscientific therapies or remedies tend to have in common. They typically claim to be effective for treating many different conditions as well as having very high success rates. The theories behind how the therapies work will often contradict much accepted scientific knowledge about how nature operates. Promoters of the therapies will tend to have little in the way of empirical evidence to support their claims, instead relying on testimonials and anecdotal reports of success. Pseudoscientific treatments for autism are often presented in a way that gives them the appearance of being scientific, such as through the use of complex jargon and perhaps with endorsements from people with academic credentials. However they are not promoted in the peer-reviewed scientific literature but instead in books, magazines and websites aimed directly at the public.

Anecdotes may be useful for providing a starting point for more in-depth scrutiny and it is possible that some anecdotal reports may be corroborated through rigorous scientific investigation. However, it has been shown that some treatments for autism which have been supported by positive testimonials and anecdotes, such as secretin and facilitated communication, have subsequently been shown to be invalid when subjected to scientific research. In particular, if there are risks associated with a treatment for autism then the evidence in support of these treatments should be particularly strong, in order to justify their use. Organisations such as ASAT (Association for Science in Autism Treatment) promote evidence-based, scientific approaches to the study and evaluation of autism interventions. The website www.researchautism.net also has a full list of all interventions and states whether they are backed up by scientific research. A list of online resources that provide a useful starting point for the appraisal of interventions for autism is provided at the end of this book.

## Summary points

- CAM treatments for autism have become popular for a number of reasons.
- There are many CAM treatments available but there is very little evidence to support their use.
- They are often based on scientifically implausible mechanisms of action.
- Some CAM treatments, such as hyperbaric oxygen therapy and chelation therapy have potentially dangerous side-effects.
- Anecdotes and personal testimonies are insufficient grounds for deciding on a treatment in the absence of evidence.

### References

1 Eisenberg, D, Davis, R, Ettner, S, Appel, S, et al. (1998) "Trends in alternative medicine use in the United States, 1990-1997." *Journal of the American Medical Association*, 280(18), pp. 1569–1575.

2 Hanson, E, Kalish, L A, Bunce, E, Curtis, C, et al. (2007) "Use of complementary and alternative medicine among children diagnosed with autism spectrum disorder." *Journal of Autism and Developmental Disorders*, 37(4), pp. 628–636.

3 Sandler, A, Brazdziunas, D and Cooley, W (2001) "Counseling families who choose complementary and alternative medicine for their child with chronic illness or disability." *Pediatrics*, 107(3), pp. 598–601.

4  Astin, J A (1998) "Why patients use alternative medecine: results of a national study." *Journal of the American Medical Association*, 279(19), pp. 1548–1553.

5  Esch, B E and Carr, J E (2004) "Secretin as a treatment for autism: a review of the evidence." *Journal of Autism and Developmental Disorders*, 34(5), pp. 543–556.

6  Marcason, W (2009) "What is the current status of research concerning use of gluten-free, casein-free diet for children diagnosed with autism?" *Journal of the American Dietetic Association*, 109(3), p. 572.

7  Millward, C, Ferriter, M, Calver, S and Connell-Jones, G (2008) "Gluten- and casein-free diets for autistic spectrum disorder." *Cochrane Database of Systematic Reviews*, (2), p. CD003498.

8  Levy, S E and Hyman, S L (2005) "Novel treatments for Autistic Spectrum Disorders." *Mental Retardation and Developmental Disabilities*, 11(2), pp. 131–142.

9  Nye, C and Brice, A (2005) "Combined vitamin B6-magnesium treatment in autism spectrum disorder." *Cochrane Database of Systematic Reviews*, (4), p. CD003497.

10  Rossignol, D A, Rossignol, L W, Smith, S, Schneider, C, et al. (2009) "Hyperbaric treatment for children with autism: a multicenter, randomized, double-blind, controlled trial." *BMC Pediatrics*, 9, p. 21.

11  Granpeesheh, D, Tarbox, J, Dixon, D R, Wilke, A E, et al. (2010) "Randomized trial of hyperbaric oxygen therapy for children with autism." *Research in Autism Spectrum Disorders*, 4(2), pp. 268–275.

12  Jepson, B, Granpeesheh, D, Tarbox, J, Olive, M L, et al. (2011) "Controlled evaluation of the effects of hyperbaric oxygen therapy on the behavior of 16 children with autism spectrum disorders." *Journal of Autism and Developmental Disorders*, 41(5), pp. 575–588.

13  Williams, P G, Hersh, J H, Allard, A and Sears, L L (2008) "A controlled study of mercury levels in hair samples of children with autism as compared to their typically developing siblings." *Research in Autism Spectrum Disorders*, 2(1), pp. 170–175.

14  Sinha, Y (2006) "Chelation therapy and autism." *British Medical Journal*, 333(7571), p. 756.

15  Davis, T N, O'Reilly, M, Kang, S, Lang, R, et al. (2013) "Chelation treatment for autism spectrum disorders: A systematic review." *Research in Autism Spectrum Disorders*, 7(1), pp. 49–55.

16  Mostert, M P (2001) "Facilitated communication since 1995: a review of published studies." *Journal of Autism and Developmental Disorders*, 31(3), pp. 287–313.

17  Jacobson, J W, Mulick, J A and Schwartz, A A (1995) "A history of facilitated communication: science, pseudoscience, and antiscience science working group on facilitated communication." *American Psychologist*, 50(9), pp. 750–765.

# Conclusion

Autism is a highly complex condition that has challenged the scientific community and stimulated a great deal of research in a variety of areas to determine its causes and the best avenues for treatment and intervention. Parallel to this, there has been an increase in levels of pseudoscientific information relating to autism. People with autism themselves and the parents of children with autism who wish to learn about the condition face a minefield of misinformation and uncritical presentation of bogus causes and treatments by the media and groups such as anti-vaccination campaigners. Having read this book, readers will come away with a good understanding of the current state of autism science research, as well as a clear idea of how to effectively evaluate various sources of information relating to autism such as websites, newspapers or television.

The next section is a list of resources that promote evidence-based autism research and which may be useful for further study.

# A number of organisations show strong support for the role of science in autism research.

The Association for Science in Autism Treatment (www.asatonline.org)has detailed explanations of the various treatments available for autism and the evidence supporting them.

The Autism Science Foundation (www.autismsciencefoundation.org) provides information about autism to the general public and describes some of the latest scientific research relating to autism.

Autistica (www.autistica.org.uk) raises and invests funds in high-quality biomedical research which focuses on determining the causes of autism, improving diagnosis and advancing new treatments and interventions.

The National Autistic Society (www.autism.org.uk) has useful general information about autism, as well as a document about the genetics of autism written for a general audience.

NICE pathway for autism (http://pathways.nice.org.uk/pathways/autism) – an easy to use tool that gives an overview of the NICE guidelines for autism.

Research Autism (www.researchautism.net) lists all interventions for autism and provides information on whether there has been any scientific research to support the use of these interventions.

# Blog sites

Internet science blogs can be a good source of information about current autism research and often disseminate the research far more effectively than do the popular press.

LBRB (leftbrainrightbrain.co.uk) – a blog dealing with autism news, science and opinion.

Cracking the Enigma (crackingtheenigma.blogspot.com) – an autism research blog.

Neurologica (theness.com/neurologicablog) – a blog on neuroscience and critical thinking that often deals with autism.

BishopBlog (deevybee.blogspot.com) – the blog of Dorothy Bishop, an Oxford-based researcher of neuroscience who often writes about autism.

Science blogs (scienceblogs.com) – collection of science blogs that often cover autism-related research.

# Books

Bad Science by Ben Goldacre. Published by Harper Collins, London – This book analyses bad science in relation to medicine and includes a chapter on the MMR health scare.

Autism's False Prophets by Paul Offit. Published by Columbia University Press – This book traces the history of the autism-vaccine controversy and describes some of the pseudoscientific treatments for autism that are used.

# Checklist: **Autism Science**

| | |
|---|---|
| Can autism be easily defined? | ✗ |
| Is autism caused by parents being emotionally unresponsive to their children? | ✗ |
| Has the number of diagnosed cases of autism been rising in the population? | ✓ |
| Do changing diagnostic criteria and increased awareness of autism play a large role in this rise? | ✓ |
| Is there a strong, complex genetic component to autism? | ✓ |
| Do the brains of people with autism develop differently from those without autism? | ✓ |
| Do most people with autism have a special talent for maths or memorisation? | ✗ |
| Do the media always present accurate coverage of autism science? | ✗ |
| Is there a large amount of misinformation relating to the causes and treatments of autism? | ✓ |
| Is rigorous scientific investigation necessary for understanding the biology of autism? | ✓ |
| Have the main environmental factors contributing to autism been identified? | ✗ |
| Do vaccines cause autism? | ✗ |
| Is there a 'cure' for autism? | ✗ |
| Is it important for a proposed treatment for autism to have strong scientific support? | ✓ |
| Can evidence-based interventions improve the quality of life of people with autism? | ✓ |

# About the Authors

## Dr. Neil Walsh

After graduating with a 1st class honours degree in the life sciences from University College Dublin, Ireland, Neil moved to the UK to undertake a PhD research project at the University of Cambridge. His studies involved using cutting-edge molecular biology technologies to investigate the genetic basis of evolutionary adaptation. Following completion of his doctoral thesis, he continued his work at Cambridge as a post-doctoral research associate. He has presented his research findings at major international molecular biology conferences and his research has been published in the Proceedings of the Royal Society.

In his current role as a Medical Writer, Neil produces a wide range of educational and technical documents for dissemination to a variety of audiences in the healthcare professions.

## Dr. Elisabeth Hurley

Dr Elisabeth Hurley spent 7 years studying Neuroscience at the University of Manchester. She has a BSc and a PhD in Neuroscience, specialising in the effect of light on the development of the body clock. After completing her PhD, she pursued her interest in autism and became the research officer at Autism West Midlands in October 2012. Her role ensures that Autism West Midlands is aware of and contributing to the most recent autism research.